WOMEN IN POLITICS

WOMEN

in

POLITICS

BREAKING DOWN
the BARRIERS *to* ACHIEVE
TRUE REPRESENTATION

MARY CHUNG
HAYASHI

Published in the United States by MKC Press,
an imprint of MKC Public Affairs, LLC.

This book is rooted in factual narratives and captures authentic experiences of women in politics. While it encompasses a broad range of stories, it may not fully encapsulate the diversity of all women's experiences due to the vast and varied nature of individual journeys in the political realm.

The Library of Congress Cataloging-in-Publication data available upon request.

ISBN 979-8-9890039-2-1 (Hardcover)
ISBN: 979-8-9890039-0-7 (Paperback)
ISBN 979-8-9890039-1-4 (eBook)

WOMEN IN POLITICS may be purchased for educational, business, or promotional use. Please contact MKC Press by email at events@mkcpress.com

Book Design by Olivia M. Hammerman

"We all have a role to play in changing the look of leadership in our world, one elected office at a time."

—MARY HAYASHI

In memory of my mom

CONTENTS

FOREWORD

My grandfather's quote, "You are so brave and quiet I forget you are suffering," profoundly reflects the essence of the book you are about to read: *Women In Politics.* The author, Mary Hayashi, has spent her life supporting a whole population who *suffer* under this spell of silence. She read this quote, digested it, understood it, and moved forward as a voice for women, especially those with mental health issues.

I come from a well-known and incredibly talented family of creatives: the Hemingways. This great heritage carries with it deep wounds, traumas and a genetic predisposition to mental illness and addiction. Throughout my younger years, I was plagued by a constant fear of succumbing to the darker aspects of my family's legacy. I worried that if I spoke out about my mental struggles, I was inviting mental illness to manifest in my life. That possibility was terrifying, and silence was my solution. Years of searching for answers about why members of my family took their lives, drank too much, or lived too hard was my secret drive.

Being a woman who came from a generation of silence was a challenge, too. It was not until I realized that we can change the trajectory of our existence by speaking out that my life shifted. Telling my story in a public forum, making a documentary, writing a book, and starting a mental health foundation has been my way to find inner peace. Mary, meanwhile, has found solace by creating legislation and advocating for the underserved in this country, and her work changes the trajectory of entire communities.

The power of a woman is inherent, but the attributes of femininity can be truly inconceivable to some males in this country, especially in the political arena. That may be why, in some parts of the business and political world, men have been trying to keep that female voice at bay. But turning a blind eye and walking away from the challenges of her femininity, her Asian American heritage, and the fact that she is deeply rooted (and hugely successful) in the political world is not how Mary Hayashi deals with issues. She faces them head on, continuing to make a difference in the world for women who are marginalized or put into boxes where they feel they cannot be heard.

I always believed that making a difference through politics was futile, but Mary Hayashi debunks that idea by demonstrating how she has used power and courage to stand up against the party line— whether political or societal—and create real change for women. She also shares her personal history of struggle and grief, having lost her oldest sister to suicide at a young age, just as I did, to which I deeply sympathize. And finally, Mary knows that shifting the way the world thinks about a problem, whether it is gender, or race, or even a political stance, takes diligence and focus. She gracefully embodies these qualities.

Women in Politics is a book that inspires women, reminding them that their voice *does* matter. But it's more than that. Mary's political and other achievements are significant not because she is a woman, but because she worked tirelessly to ensure their importance. As a result, these accomplishments have become life-altering solutions for women.

Even more beautiful: Mary Hayashi is not finished. I look forward to seeing where her strength and courage will take her in the future.

—MARIEL HEMINGWAY, Actress and Author

PART I

INSPIRATION

CHAPTER 1

MY JOURNEY

"You can't be what you can't see."

—JENNIFER SIEBEL NEWSOME's documentary *Miss Representation*, quoting Marian Wright Edelman, Founder and President Emerita of the Children's Defense Fund

One of my first experiences in public office is a powerful reminder that we can make a lasting difference in individual lives through public service.

In the spring of 2007, not long after I was elected to the California State Assembly, I met Jacqueline Coats. Her husband, Marlin Coats—a United States citizen and former lifeguard—drowned on May 14, 2006. He was caught in a riptide at San Francisco's Ocean Beach while helping rescue two brothers, ages eleven and fourteen, who were struggling in the surf. Marlin was twenty-nine years old at the time.

Here's what happened: Marlin was celebrating Mother's Day with his family on the beach when he heard the two young boys shout for help. He removed his shoes and swam out to rescue them. He was successful in rescuing the older boy, but when he returned to help the younger boy, he was submerged. Two lifeguards pulled him and the younger boy out of the water to safety, but Marlin could not be revived. He had drowned.

Marlin and his wife, Jacqueline, a legal immigrant from Kenya, were in the middle of permanent residency proceedings for Jacqueline when Marlin died. Jacqueline was a constituent, living in San Leandro at the time, but Marlin's death voided the residency proceedings. If an immigrant's American spouse dies within the first two years of marriage, before the application is processed, US immigration policy dictates that their green card request will be rejected. That meant that by the time I heard about Jacqueline's plight, deportation efforts were already underway.

This wasn't the first time Jacqueline had faced deportation. Jacqueline came to the United States in 2001 to attend San Jose State University, where she first met Marlin Coats. Marlin was a family-oriented man, and Jacqueline was always part of Marlin's family gatherings at Christmas and Thanksgiving celebrations. Two years after they met, they married. But eleven days before the wedding, deportation proceedings began. Immigration officials had been notified that though Jacqueline had been taking classes, she was still three units short of what was required. This technicality had caused her to lose her legal immigration status.

After the wedding, Marlin Coats petitioned for residency in his wife's name, and because she had entered the United States legally, she was able to stay in the country. Those papers were prepared and ready for submission when Marlin died while saving the two boys in San Francisco's Ocean Beach in 2006.

In January of 2007, several California congressional members filed a bill requesting Congress to allow Jacqueline's legal status, but it failed passage. When Jacqueline reached out to my district office for help, I began to look for ways to allow Jacqueline to continue seeking permanent status. Eventually, I launched a letter-writing campaign to Senator Dianne Feinstein, asking her to introduce a private bill for Jacqueline Coats.

A private bill provides benefits to specific individuals, but because only a US Senator can introduce one, this solution is typically reserved for when administrative or legal remedies have been exhausted. Still, I knew that many private bills deal with immigration matters, granting citizenship or permanent residency. As long as the private bill was introduced and pending in Congress, Jacqueline would be allowed to legally remain in the United States.

After several months of letter-writing campaigns, I received a call from Senator Dianne Feinstein's office. The message was that she would like to meet with Jacqueline Coats and me at her San Francisco residence to discuss our request. I was thrilled. When we met with Senator Feinstein, she was incredibly supportive and offered to help in any way she could. Soon, the private bill was introduced, and Jacqueline was able to petition US Immigration and Customs Enforcement for further consideration of her unique situation.

I learned a lot from Jacqueline Coats, like the injustice often inherent in our laws, the extraordinary heroism and perseverance that exist in ordinary people, and about making the system work for us instead of against us.

HOW I GOT THERE

Growing up, I never imagined myself as a civic leader. As a young girl named Mi Kyung in the 1970s farming village of Gwangju, South Korea, I had no concept of representative democracy.

Nestled in a river basin and surrounded by high mountains, Gwangju was an enchanting place to grow up. On clear winter days, my older sister and I would ice skate on the Geukrak River. Skating was one of our favorite pastimes, and though there were safer places to skate, our first choice was always the river.

Gwangju called itself "The City of Hope," but its natural beauty hid a tumultuous history of failed pro-democracy movements. The most famous of these was the 1980 Gwangju Uprising, where the students of Chonnam University and Gwangju's citizens protested General Chun Doo Hwan's assumption of power and use of martial law.[1] The unrest lasted nine days, during which time students were killed, raped, and assaulted by the government military. Official records place the death toll at 170, but the real numbers are likely higher.

Though the people of my hometown strove for freedom, I couldn't fathom a world where every citizen had an equal voice or where people elected their peers to represent them. Even further from my mind was the idea that a woman might serve in such a role. The only roles women were expected to perform—or, more accurately, *allowed* to perform—were maintaining the home and caring for their families.

In traditional Korean culture, women are to be seen and not heard. We are each raised to be respectful "good girls," to make an excellent marriage match, and then to raise children: a new generation of silent "good girls." My father and his mother were committed to raising my sisters and me accordingly; being good meant keeping my thoughts and opinions to myself. Any direct communication—even direct eye contact—was discouraged, and avoiding conflict altogether was expected.

In the sleepy town of Gwangju, everyone knew each other. This meant I constantly had to be on my best behavior should reports make their way back to my parents and grandmother. There was no "I," only "we," and we had to be good or we would shame the entire family. As a result, my sisters and I shouldered the heavy burden of being perfect.

Fortunately, my sisters and I excelled at being "good girls," and regular reports from the townspeople stating so brought my parents great pride. I was happy to oblige. It felt good to please my parents and to have their approval. In our homogenous Korean culture, especially in our small farming village, I wasn't exposed to any other way of life. As a result, this limited "good girl" upbringing set barriers around my imagination.

That is, until we moved to America, and my eyes were opened.

After years of political discord and various failed attempts at administrative reintegration with its northern neighbor, on August 15, 1948, South Korea became an independent country. In the decades that followed, South Korea experienced fluctuating periods of democratic and autocratic rule. The only thing that thwarted repeated attempts to establish a military dictatorship was a series of protests, often led by young male college students. These included the student revolt in 1960 that ended the reign of South Korea's first president, Syngman Rhee; the assassination of third president, Park Chung-hee, spurred by anti-government demonstrations; and, as previously mentioned, the Gwangju Uprising. Recognizing the rising political turmoil, my parents decided that we would be safer living in another country.

Being a twelve-year-old girl is hard enough, but being a twelve-year-old girl suddenly dropped in a foreign land, where I didn't speak the language or understand the culture, was an entirely different level of challenge. When my parents decided to move us to America in 1980, we were far from the only ones fleeing political unrest and ongoing threats of danger; in fact, the Korean population in the United States increased from 11,000 in 1960 to 290,000 in 1980.[2] So we weren't alone, but it often felt that way.

My parents gave my siblings and me new American names. I was no longer Mi Kyung; from that moment forward, I was Mary. I was also one of only five non-white children at Hewes Junior High School in Orange County. I was entirely unable to communicate or develop genuine relationships of any kind. By that point in my life, my "good girl" training was firmly ingrained, so I chose to be silent. I became invisible.

After six months of merely surviving, my math teacher sent me to the school's office. I had struggled to explain math problems on the blackboard, as she had directed. I understood the math, of course, but I needed a better command of English to present my thoughts. At the office, another Korean boy came to translate for me, and I finally had a chance to make myself heard. I poured my heart out to the poor boy, who kindly translated my distress to the school's staff. I felt relieved. Fortunately, after that, the school secured an English tutor for me, and things became more accessible. Still, I downplayed and even hid most of this from my parents. They viewed a need for assistance as a sign of weakness—the same reason they hadn't proactively secured help for me to learn English in the first place.

As my English continued to improve, I assimilated more into American culture. I even became exposed to the Asian American subculture and observed Asian Americans in different roles. For example, I idolized Connie Chung and her regular appearances on the evening news. Here was a woman who looked like me yet was doing more than simply marrying and raising children. She was educated, articulate, and, as far as I could tell, quite powerful. The barrier around my imagination was lifting, and I was starting to see new options for myself.

After a few more years of assimilation, I was a full-blown American girl. In high school, I wore makeup (that I put on at school so my parents wouldn't see), tried (and failed) to dye my hair blonde, and even went to prom. While my father desperately continued trying to impose our Korean culture, traditions, and values, he could see that I was far more American than Korean.

In 1986, I was a college freshman at California State University, Long Beach, and Women's Empowerment was at a peak. Madonna's "Like A Virgin" was number one on Billboard's charts, Margaret Atwood's *The Handmaid's Tale* hit bookshelves everywhere, Geraldine Ferraro was the first woman candidate for Vice President of the United States, and EMILY's List was founded, with the strategic mission to see more pro-choice women elected to political office. In American homes, more and more mothers were holding down full-time jobs and even building successful careers. Little girls were being told that they, too, could and should pursue education to have a career of their choosing.

As a young college student, I wasn't overly aware of the advancement of women happening all around me; I was focused instead on forging my independence from my parents. They had decided to move back to South Korea with my younger siblings because of my father's concerns about our family losing its Korean roots. At that time, I was nineteen years old and a US citizen. I convinced my parents to let me remain in Southern California, where I lived alone in the house they kept.

But my parents maintained a firm hold on me, even from the other side of the world. During my first trip home to visit, they introduced me to a young man whom my father had arranged for me to marry. I was twenty years old, and the man—who we called by his American name, Hunter—was twenty-seven years old. The "good girl" in me went along with the plan for several months, unsure whether I could or even wanted to push back. While Asian parents are typically strong advocates for education, my parents' focus there extended exclusively to my brothers; my sisters and I were only encouraged to go to school long enough to marry someone intelligent and wealthy—before we were twenty-one and over the hill.

At the same time, I signed up for a Women's Studies class, thinking that I would be studying how to be a "good woman," just as I had learned how to be a "good girl." Instead, I read countless stories about fiercely independent women written by great feminists like Virginia Woolf and Sylvia Plath. After years of being a "good girl," of being raised with the notion that I would be nothing more than a wife and mother, and after assimilating to a new culture where women were allowed to have their own lives and pursue careers, it finally dawned on me: I didn't have to marry Hunter. I didn't have to clean my parents' house every night when I got home from classes as if they were still living there. Most importantly, I realized I could make a career for myself and make a difference for others.

Inspired by the authors from my Women's Studies class—women who enlightened me about the vast array of opportunities available to me—I aim to enlighten today's women about our potential in politics through this book. It is crucial for us to understand not only our history as a gender but also our present standing and the milestones we need to reach to achieve true equality in this country.

THE CASE FOR INCREASED REPRESENTATION OF WOMEN IN POLITICS

The United States government operates as a representative democracy, which requires all its citizens to be represented for it to function effectively. Yet, the importance of electing more women to government positions is still not entirely acknowledged. To address this issue, Political Parity, a nonpartisan research organization, has begun the important work of documenting women's contributions in government. Among the key findings of their groundbreaking study *Representation Matters* is that women's legislative priorities in Congress are influenced by their personal and professional experiences and identities. A number of women in this study said they view themselves as a "voice for the voiceless," so they represent children's issues and economically disadvantaged people whose interests may have been historically overlooked. These women in Congress also expressed their commitment to representing their districts or states regardless of who may have voted for them.[3]

A CBS News article highlighting the record number of women running for governor in November 2022 featured a quote from Massachusetts Attorney General Maura Healey, who said, "I believe that representation matters. We will have more effective laws and policies and government when we have those in government elected to serve better reflect the diversity of our population."[4] Maura Healey was the first openly gay attorney general for Massachusetts and, later that same month, became its first female governor.

The article notes Maura's observation that many women make financial decisions for their families and households. For this reason, Maura ran her 2022 gubernatorial campaign on a platform of family economics, such as affordable housing, transportation, and childcare. She was also the first Massachusetts attorney general to adopt paid parental leave for the state. Maura's family-focused policies and candidacy perfectly demonstrate the effectiveness of a government for the people, by the people—which includes women.

Furthermore, research has shown that having more women in positions of power promotes global health. A study published in *SSM—Population Health* found that significant advancements in healthcare access, educational opportunities, and women's rights correlate with more women serving in government.[5]

Research also suggests that women legislators excel at bringing more resources back to their home districts. Sarah Anzia and Christopher Berry, the authors of a study published in the *American Journal of Political Science*, found that congresswomen secure roughly 9 percent more spending from federal discretionary programs than congressmen. They also found that women sponsor and co-sponsor significantly more legislation than their male counterparts.[6]

So, if representation is the foundation of the United States government and more women in power benefit us all, why are women still *under*represented in our elected offices? What creates such disparity after generations of supposed equality?

BREAKING BARRIERS

While we celebrate the accomplishments of women, it's crucial to remember the longstanding systemic gender discrimination women have faced. Generations of cultural, systemic, and racial barriers won't dissolve overnight. We're in the midst of a profound, yet still unfolding transition.

Viewing this transition through a historical lens underscores the magnitude of what we still need to overcome. In California, for example, only 192 women have served in the state's legislature since 1911, when women were first allowed to hold office. This is out of over 4,497 total California state legislators. With this context, we're reminded that while the numbers might improve, we have generations of inequality to compensate for.

Despite tremendous gains in women's representation in powerful leadership positions, a significant number of people across the world still do not trust women as influential leaders. A report by the Wilson Center, a nonpartisan, congressionally chartered organization that provides research and analysis of global affairs issues, states, "Public perceptions regarding women's ability to lead is a key driver of how much power they will have while in office."[7] The Reykjavik Index assesses attitudes toward female leadership in the G7 countries—Canada, France, Germany, Italy, Japan, the UK, and the US—as well as India, Kenya, and Nigeria. The 2020/2021 Reykjavik Index for Leadership found that only 41 percent of people in Germany and 38 percent of people in Japan said they felt very comfortable with a woman being the head of government.[8]

The remnants of centuries of gender inequality are still very much around us. There is not one single glass ceiling that women in politics need to break through to succeed. In truth, we are faced with numerous barriers blocking our path to power: financial, cultural, racial, and social. We must apply our creativity and grit to climb over them, crawl under them, and go around them anyway we can—and then turn around and lend a helping hand to the women coming behind us. The journey requires momentum, tenacity, and resilience; it's not just one magic moment.

The biggest barrier of all is the barrier in our imagination. Just as my "good girl" training as a child in Korea limited my imagination, so too has our societal "good girl" training limited our collective imagination of what women can do, be, and achieve. In this book, I hope to provide insight into the many facets of my life as a girl growing up in Korea; as an Asian American immigrant; as a survivor who lost her older sister to suicide; as a national health care advocate; as an elected official; and as an advocate for women's rights. Each of these parts of my life has provided its own challenges, lessons, successes, and struggles, and the sum of these experiences has made me who I am.

Throughout this book, I'll also discuss the various barriers that keep women from achieving full political parity and how others have overcome them. The electoral environment is highly competitive and full of biases against women, but these barriers are not insurmountable. The motivations, the journey, and the rewards of public service are inherently different for women than for men, but that shouldn't keep us from taking our place. Despite the odds, thousands of women have found ways to hold office and make a difference, getting us closer to a true representative democracy.

I am honored to have interviewed many of these inspiring women leaders for this book: Karen Bass, Lauren Book, Laphonza Butler, Sue Chan, Rosemary Dyer, Jean Fuller, Cathleen Galgiani, Giselle Hale, Dallas Harris, Amanda Hunter, Celinda Lake, Sally Lieber, Fiona Ma, Sunny Mojonnier, Sandy Pappas, Connie Perez-Andreesen, Lisa Reynolds, and Cindy Ryu. In these pages, you will read about what motivated them to run for public office and how they've made a difference. You'll also discover stories and insights from professionals I've collaborated with, including Darrell Steinberg, my mentor. These men and women come from all walks of life—they have different ages, backgrounds, political affiliations, and levels of ambition—but they all demonstrate that each of us has a vital role to play in our country's political system.

I hope these stories will serve as a resource and inspiration to others who want to change the world—one elected office at a time. With so many issues still very much at stake for American women—from equal pay to reproductive rights—we can't afford *not* to participate.

CHAPTER 2

THE POWER OF VOICE

"You are so brave and quiet; I forget you are suffering."
—ERNEST HEMINGWAY

Our lives are shaped by a collection of moments, defining memories that determine who we are and what we choose to do and why. Often, those memories are a call to action. When we heed them, we have the potential to create an impact above and beyond what we ever imagined. Countless women in power have heeded such calls to action, and their unique experiences and perspectives have reshaped our world.

Bo Yoon is my defining memory.

As a young girl, I intensely looked up to my oldest sister, Bo Yoon. She was tall, pretty, popular, and a "good girl" by all accounts. I remember when my family moved into a great big house in Seoul in 1978, I was ecstatic that Bo Yoon and I would still share a room.

No one in our family knew that young, vibrant Bo Yoon was troubled. Perhaps the pressure of being a "good girl" was too much, or perhaps she felt stifled in a life destined for nothing more than marrying and having children. Unfortunately, no one will ever know because on January 1, 1980, at the precious age of seventeen, Bo Yoon took her own life.

The morning of her suicide, she showed me an empty bottle of sleeping pills she had consumed the night before, and she alluded to some desperate act she was going to perform. But in my twelve-year-old world, I couldn't comprehend her cry for help. So, instead of doing something, I visited my friend's house.

Later that day, my cousin, Soon Oak, called to say I needed to come home. After making my way home in a daze, knowing that something terrible had happened, I learned that my older brother had found Bo Yoon hanging in our bedroom.

After that day, no one spoke of Bo Yoon again. There was no memorial service and no burial. We never talked about her death or why it possibly happened. My siblings and I were left with nothing but our memories, which were hard to hold onto considering Bo Yoon was cropped from all family photos and all her belongings were disposed of. My parents attempted to erase all signs that she had ever existed.

In hindsight, I understand that they didn't have any other choice. At that time and in that place, there were no tools or resources for managing mental health issues or coping with a tragedy like teenage suicide. Instead, the fact that a family member committed such an act was viewed as a shameful embarrassment to be hidden, not a tragic incident to be understood and mourned. Bo Yoon had, knowingly or unknowingly, performed the greatest act of rebellion against her "good girl" orders. The only way forward for my parents was to sweep it under the rug and pretend that the whole ordeal—and my sister—never happened.

While my parents might have been able to suffer in silence, I could not. My involvement in public service grew organically out of my innate desire to fight for those who were falling behind, being forgotten, or unable to advocate for themselves—for people just like my sister.

FINDING MY VOICE

In 1990, at twenty-three years old, I was living in the San Francisco Bay Area, in an eight hundred square foot apartment that became my sanctuary. There, finally out from under my parents' rule, Bo Yoon's memory was at the forefront of my mind and the top of my heart. I never stopped wondering why she made the choice that she did.

During that time, I attended the University of San Francisco in the evenings to complete my bachelor's degree. I worked at the Asian Law Caucus, a national civil rights legal organization. I also became involved in numerous organizations working to advance women's rights. With my newfound freedom and a clear view of my potential, I decided to dedicate myself to making a difference and empowering others to do the same.

In the early 1990s, there was a great void in the Asian American community concerning women's health advocacy. Not only did I need to learn more about why Bo Yoon couldn't ask for help, I also wanted to do something to help others who were similarly struggling with mental illness. I refused to forget those who were suffering, and I wasn't going to let others forget about them, either. It was the beginning of my lifelong advocacy for mental health and my passion for improving the overall health of Asian women in America.

It was an exciting time in San Francisco; there seemed to be a nonprofit organization for every cause imaginable. Barely ten years into my life in the United States, I enthusiastically absorbed all of it, meeting countless individuals who further inspired me to make a difference. In 1993, for example, I met Elizabeth Toledo, the San Francisco Chapter President of the National Organization for Women (and later, the organization's vice president). Though

I was going to school at night and working full-time during the day, I always made time to volunteer for Elizabeth. I still have vivid memories of stuffing envelopes with donation request letters for her organization.

Elizabeth was a fervent advocate for change, and we quickly bonded over our shared passion for women's issues. She seemed perfect: independent, well-spoken, and passionate about women's rights. I viewed her as a role model and mentor even though she was only five years older than me.

In April 1996, Elizabeth invited me to speak at a march in San Francisco, organized by the National Organization for Women (NOW). After Reverend Jesse Jackson addressed the men and women who had gathered to "Fight the Radical Right," I spoke on stage about the importance of Asian American women's health. Gloria Steinem stood right next to me, applauding my words along with the crowd of thirty-thousand.

Those few years I spent learning from powerful female leaders were my most formative, and they shaped me into the leader I am today. They showed me how to organize for a cause, how to network with others, and how to embrace the power of one's voice. I was part of something larger than me, and it was incredible.

But those years also showed me that, while there were many powerful female leaders in the African American and Latina communities, there was a dearth of representation for Asian American women. So, although I had no idea where to begin and had only three years of experience working for a nonprofit organization, I decided to take the next significant step for Bo Yoon and all the voiceless Asian women and families. In 1993, I founded the National Asian Women's Health Organization (NAWHO).

Though I began with no resources of any kind, I received enormous support from feminists like Elizabeth Toledo and Byllye Avery, founder of the National Black Women's Health Project. Both women agreed there should be a national voice for Asian American women's health issues, and they introduced me to potential donors and political supporters. They also invited me to serve on leadership boards, where I learned invaluable advocacy skills.

During the next few years, I grew NAWHO into an organization of thousands, all of whom were committed to ending healthcare disparity among ethnic and racial groups in America. Through engagement efforts like our National Leadership Training Network, which brought several hundred of Asian American health care advocates to Washington DC, we helped shape public policy for those who would have otherwise gone unrepresented.

MENTAL HEALTH CHAMPION

In 2001, I moved from the San Francisco Bay Area to Sacramento to be with my future husband, and I began looking for new employment. I wanted to keep doing my part in making changes that would improve the lives of others, and my chance came when I met Darrell Steinberg, who is currently serving as Mayor of Sacramento. As a California assemblymember at the time, he had co-founded the Capitol Unity Council (CUC) in 1998 in response to a series of hate crimes in Sacramento, California. These malicious acts of violence included the murder of a gay couple and fire bomb attacks on the offices of the Japanese American Citizens League, the NAACP, three synagogues, a women's health clinic, and the home of Sacramento's Asian American vice mayor.

When I first moved, CUC was a new non-profit that was just getting its feet off the ground. At the time, it was experiencing unstable operational management. My friends, social justice advocate Leticia Alejandrez and then-Senator Deborah Ortiz, were on the CUC board, and they asked if I would be interested in helping to develop long-term strategies to ensure the success of the organization's goals. Naturally, the program piqued my interest. Since Leticia and Deborah knew of my work in gender equality, diversity, and non-profit organization development, they asked me to meet with Darrell. After a short interview, he hired me as the executive director of CUC.

Darrell was a vocal advocate for increasing the scope and availability of mental health programs. During his first term in the state assembly, he authored AB34, which authorized pilot projects to provide integrated services to the homeless population in three counties. This pilot program evaluation showed success in reducing hospitalization and incarceration. Then, in 2004, he teamed up with Rusty Selix, a longtime mental health leader and lobbyist, to write Proposition 63. This groundbreaking Mental Health Services Act would impose a 1 percent tax on incomes of $1,000,000 to fund mental health programs; a portion of that money would be dedicated to prevention and early intervention programs focused on detecting and treating mental illness before it becomes debilitating.

During the Proposition 63 mental health initiative campaign, Darrell often talked about the impact of Governor Ronald Reagan's decision to drastically cut services to mentally ill people by closing state hospitals. Reagan had promised that mentally ill people would be treated in more compassionate settings in community-based facilities, but that promise was never realized. As a result, thousands of people ended up homeless and incapable of caring for themselves. California desperately needed additional resources for its mental health system and new resources for early intervention and prevention programs.

I asked Darrell if I could help, given my interest in mental health, and was assigned as the Alameda County Coordinator for the Proposition 63 campaign. Our initial funding came from the California Hospital Association and the Service Employees International Union, California affiliate. Then, the mayor at the time, Gavin Newsom, endorsed the ballot measure, providing us with the momentum and visibility we really needed. In addition, through my connections from NAWHO, I secured actress Mariel Hemingway to headline a fundraiser for Proposition 63. That was one of the most successful fundraisers the campaign has ever held.

Of course, the countless individuals touched by mental illness and healthcare activists who volunteered and supported the campaign made a huge difference. Early on, I traveled with Darrell to Fresno, California, and other parts of the state where we thought the campaign could use some extra help with convincing voters to support the ballot measure. For example, Central Valley, California voters were perceived as more conservative, so we thought they might not support increased taxes, even on the wealthy millionaires. But what we learned was that many people had personal connections to mental illness—often a family member, friend, or someone they knew was silently suffering or lacked access to treatment. This personal connection was a key factor in passing this critical mental health ballot measure.

In November 2004, on a statewide ballot, this measure was approved by 54 percent of California voters. It was such an exciting time for all those who had worked so hard for mental health, and we celebrated this tremendous victory for a cause that had been so stigmatized and silenced. Through its passage, the proposition created the Mental Health Services Act, providing unprecedented funding for county mental health services to expand and improve care for children and adults in need.

Shortly after the passage of Proposition 63, Governor Arnold Schwarzenegger appointed me to serve as a commissioner to the California Mental Health Services Oversight and Accountability Commission, which monitored and guided the state's implementation of Proposition 63. Since 2005, Proposition 63 has generated twenty-nine billion dollars for mental health programs.

The Proposition 63 experience opened my eyes to new ways I could make an impact. Darrell used his platform as a legislator to do much more than author legislation and work on the state's budget; he used his position to advance causes he deeply cared about. After seeing firsthand what Darrell was able to achieve, I was inspired to move from an advocate influencing legislators to a legislator with the power to implement change.

Shortly after the passage of Proposition 63, I decided to run for California State Assembly, and on December 4, 2006, I took office as State Assemblymember for California's eighteenth district. The first Korean American woman to serve in the California State Legislature, I authored several bills focused on mental health, including AB 509, which required the establishment of California's first Office of Suicide Prevention.

VOICES FOR THE VOICELESS

I join a powerful chorus of voices compelled to serve.

At thirty-seven, Lauren Book, an articulate mother of two, has already made a name for herself as a Democratic minority leader. In 2016, she was elected to the Florida Senate's thirty-second district seat after running unopposed. During our interview, she said that she, like me, was inspired to run for public office because she wanted to be a voice for the voiceless. Unfortunately, her path, too, was a distressing one.

Because Lauren's mother suffered from mental illness and her father often traveled for work, Lauren and her two siblings were frequently looked after by caregivers. A new nanny began working for the family in August of 1994, when Lauren was ten years old. In December, that nanny sexually abused Lauren for the first time. Because Lauren did not disclose the incident, the nanny continued preying on Lauren, often with her parents just down the hall. Sometimes, her brother was even in the same room. This abuse happened almost daily and continued until Lauren was seventeen years old.

Lauren's experience was horrendous. For seven of the most precious years of her life, she was imprisoned by powerlessness and constant fear.

Lauren eventually disclosed the abuse to her highly supportive father, and he immediately took action. The nanny was arrested and convicted of child abuse.

Lauren's advocate at the time implored her to get tested for HIV. Though a negative test result was reassuring, it was also unreliable, as the virus can live dormant and not appear on a blood test. That meant the only way to be certain was to test the nanny, but there was no way to compel Lauren's assailant to take the test. So, Lauren and her father took further action, approaching a legislator to author a bill that would change state law and make such testing mandatory. During the closing days of the 2003 legislative session, the Florida state legislature passed legislation that gave survivors of sexual assault the right to require testing of their assailants for sexually transmitted diseases, with the results provided within forty-eight hours.

The experience opened Lauren's eyes to just how impactful the legislative process can be. The change in the law meant that she—and other victims of abuse—would have faster access to medical treatment. This was a real change that impacted her, and it left an impression.[9]

As she completed extensive counseling and began to heal, Lauren realized that she could use her traumatic experience to help others. After working in advocacy—and with the encouragement of her father, whose career in politics had demonstrated to Lauren how impactful public service could be—Lauren decided to run for office.

Through her years of service to survivors of abuse, Lauren has successfully advocated for the passage of more than two dozen state and national laws to protect victims and keep predators at bay, including the nation's toughest mandatory reporting laws, legislation that created Children's Safety Zones, and laws ending the statute of limitations for the prosecution of sexual crimes committed against children.[10]

"When you go so long in your life without a voice, you can't stand by while others remain voiceless." Lauren was driven to public service because she felt compelled to fight for victims who couldn't fight for themselves. She wanted to help those who suffered through similar trauma as she had and, ideally, to prevent such tragedies from happening in the first place.

Cathleen Galgiani's story is different from Lauren's and mine, but it reveals a similar call to action and a desire to shape change. When Cathleen was seventeen, her nineteen-year-old cousin went missing. Cathleen's family spent what little resources they had to locate the young woman, to no avail. There wasn't much the local authorities could do, and the case remains unsolved. Throughout the process, Cathleen learned more than she ever expected to learn about victims' rights and how poorly missing person cases were handled.

"I was haunted by the fact that as long as my cousin remained missing, her case would not be treated as a crime," Cathleen reflected. In 2014, she introduced California Senate Bill 1066, which, among other changes, expanded the treatment of young missing person cases from those under sixteen to those under twenty-one years of age. It also provided greater flexibility in how missing persons could be reported.[11] "I felt like, since I could not bring my cousin home, at least I could help improve the chances for others who'd lost someone they loved." Like Lauren and me, Cathleen has heard her call to public service as fighting for those who can't fight for themselves.

People often underestimate Cathleen. She is a former beauty pageant queen with platinum blonde hair and a soft demeanor. However, throughout her career, she has stood up to the powerful on behalf of the powerless. In 2015, for example, Cathleen filed a motion against the San Joaquin Sheriff's Office in federal court to vacate a protective order on information pertinent to five different missing person cases. She challenged the department, claiming that they were deliberately deleting and canceling DNA records and files from the national database of missing persons. With emails in hand that proved her claim, the Department of Justice ultimately restored most of the files.[12]

While women like Lauren, Cathleen, and me were called to service because of personal loss and a desire to help those facing similar difficulties, we also act as a voice for the voiceless by focusing on those who have not been historically represented in legislative bodies. Studies have shown that female lawmakers are more likely to focus on bills that impact women and children, authoring more legislation than men on issues like education, reproductive rights, equal pay, and health care.[13] Lauren's political platform is built upon advocacy for women and families; one example of her work is Florida Senate Bill 246, which she introduced to eliminate sales tax on baby diapers.[14] Such small yet impactful changes go a long way to alleviate the pressure felt by millions of Floridian families who struggle daily with the decision to put food on the table, gas in the car, or clean diapers on the baby.

Sometimes, however, this focus on social programs can penalize us politically. Because of our dedication to supporting and passing legislation focused on social programs, women are often underestimated in other areas of policy, such as the economy, defense, or business. Our credibility as candidates can even be challenged if we seem "over-focused" on family or marginalized issues.

But the assumption that women aren't as capable as men because we tend to work more for social programs is unfounded and ironic. The role of government is to serve its people, which is precisely what women do when we speak up for those who desperately need our representation. So when we propose bills that bring more equity to the vast disparities around this country, we are fulfilling the very purpose of our government. Whether through the lens of business or more overt social programs, the end goal is to improve the lives of as many citizens as possible.

CUMULATIVE EFFECTS CREATE CHANGE

It's so easy to underestimate the act of speaking up, of giving a voice to the voiceless in small ways. It's easy to dismiss it or say "it isn't worth it," especially when such actions take bravery and perseverance. But each act of speaking up adds to the conversation, until a ripple becomes a wave that becomes a storm, and the world is forever altered.

In 2006, activist Tarana Burke set up the nonprofit Just Be Inc. for young and vulnerable Black women and girls. In 2005, she introduced the term "MeToo" to help these women find a voice to talk about their sexual abuse.[15] More than a decade later, in 2017, when allegations of sexual abuse by Harvey Weinstein broke in the media, actress Alyssa Milano sent out a post on Twitter with #MeToo, calling for women and men who had been sexually assaulted or harassed to respond to her tweet with their experiences. The hashtag exploded, and the change that started with Tarana Burke spread into a global movement.

The #MeToo movement forever changed the political landscape. In April of 2018, the Barbara Lee Family Foundation released new polling information about voters' attitudes toward the #MeToo movement and how this issue would impact their voting decisions. The poll found that 81 percent of voters saw sexual harassment in the workplace as a serious problem, with 44 percent saying it is a very serious problem. 52 percent of voters decidedly agreed they would never vote for a person accused of sexual harassment. Among millennial women, 86 percent indicated that workplace sexual harassment is a serious problem, with 65 percent stating they would never vote for someone who didn't make sexual harassment a priority in the campaign. 79 percent of men in the survey considered sexual harassment in the workplace to be a serious problem, and 53 percent of men agreed they would never vote for someone accused of sexual harassment.[16]

The poll makes it clear that political candidates can no longer ignore sexual harassment and gender-based violence issues.

This change didn't happen overnight, and it involved numerous women speaking up, again and again, even when speaking up didn't always result in the change they desired. For example, in 2013, then-Michigan Senator Gretchen Whitmer gave a senate floor speech in which she argued against a bill that required women to get separate insurance for abortions, even when the pregnancy was a consequence of rape or incest. In that speech, she disclosed that she was a rape survivor.[17] Unfortunately, the bill she was trying to defeat passed the Senate.

In 2018, after the #MeToo movement surged in the public consciousness, Gretchen Whitmer was elected governor of Michigan.

"I'm here to lend my voice to this movement and encourage others to do that," she said during her gubernatorial campaign. "Because it's only by talking about the issues that we face every day that we can actually solve them."[18]

Giving voice to the voiceless always has an impact, whether for a state, or a group of people, or even the one lone person that needed you to speak up for them when they couldn't. Never underestimate this power.

STEP UP

Women like Cathleen and Lauren are called to serve a purpose. Some might say that this calling is due to women's innate caretaker qualities. Others might say it's in response to our desire to help those who are similarly underrepresented. Whatever spurs us to take the leap, we find our passion in serving others.

"I grew up watching my father—a Florida lobbyist—go to Tallahassee every week, and I developed a great appreciation for the political process at an early age. I love everything about the cadence, the rhythm of it all," Lauren told me. At the time of her first legislative session, she was thirty-two years old, and her newborn twins were just two weeks old. "I went to the capital with my c-section stitches still in, breastfeeding and pumping around the clock, and battling postpartum depression. Still, I loved every minute of it."

We each hear and feel the call to be advocates for those without a voice, albeit in different ways. Many female legislators and representatives share this urge to step up and champion the underserved and underrepresented in this country. Our contributions are significant. Our participation in the process is necessary.

Years after discovering my independence, and forty-two years after Bo Yoon's death, it's safe to say that I am no longer the "good girl" she and I were raised to be. I've learned to speak up for myself and others and not remain silent in the face of injustice. New generations of American women have been raised with a better message: rather than being taught to be a "good girl," they are told it's okay to speak up. They've been taught that women can lead, too. In fact, they're encouraged to do so.

We need more voices to speak up for the voiceless, so if you similarly hear the call to lead, I encourage you to listen.

CHAPTER 3

REPRESENTATION MATTERS

"Women belong in all the places where decisions are being made."

—RUTH BADER GINSBURG

In 1985, Rosemary Dyer took the life of her husband, David, who had spent the entirety of their eight-year marriage physically and emotionally torturing her. She shot him with the same gun he'd used to threaten and physically abuse her, but during her trial, she was not allowed to bring evidence of the abuse before the jury. In 1988, she was convicted of murder and sentenced to life without parole.

Rosemary is not an outlier, and millions of women are abused daily in the US. In 2021, the World Health Organization estimated that about one in three women worldwide had experienced either physical or sexual partner violence in their lifetime.

Securing justice is not always easy for survivors of physical violence. Just like mental health issues, violence against women can be stigmatizing. As a result, many women experience cultural pressure to hide the abuse and stay in marriages with their abusers. Others seek freedom but find no route for escape, leaving them stuck in horrifying situations until they are pushed, by years of trauma and pain, to defend themselves. Many, like Rosemary, find themselves imprisoned for the murder of their abusive partner.

In 1989, several women serving sentences in California for the murder of their abusers banded together to form Convicted Women Against Abuse (CWAA), an inmate-led group where members share their stories and discuss their legal cases. Membership eventually grew to roughly sixty inmates. In 1992, after years of letter-writing campaigns and outreach, the CWAA successfully exerted pressure on California lawmakers, leading to the recognition of "Battered Women's Syndrome" as a viable defense in the state's courts of law.

Under this defense, battered women who killed and were convicted after 1992 began receiving, on average, a six- to eight-year sentence of involuntary manslaughter instead of the murder sentences that the CWAA women had received.[19] This change dramatically altered the lives of women who had suffered and been pushed to the brink by their abusers. But for the many women who were convicted *before* 1992, including Rosemary Dyer, this defense came too late. So, once again, the incarcerated women took a stand, this time for their improper convictions.

On January 1, 2002, California Penal Code 1473.5 became law, making California the first state in the nation to permit battered women convicted of killing their abusers to file a writ of habeas corpus challenging their original conviction if sentencing occurred before 1992. In the following years, many CWAA members were released after their cases were re-tried and their convictions overturned. Unfortunately, many women remained incarcerated because they did not meet the requirement of "expert testimony" or evidence to warrant a re-trial. Rosemary Dyer was one of the many women stuck in this situation.

Enter: Fiona Ma.

I met Fiona in 2006 while campaigning to represent Oakland and other East Bay cities for the California State Assembly. Now the California state treasurer, Fiona was a San Francisco County supervisor and a dynamic, energetic, savvy candidate for state assembly in a neighboring district. She was a formidable campaigner, and I instantly loved her style. We quickly became friends.

Fiona's parents are Chinese immigrants, and her paternal grandfather, Lieutenant General Ma Zhen, served as the mayor of Kunming, Yunnan. Fiona's maternal grandfather, meanwhile, was a minister in China, Toronto, Canada, New York City, and San Francisco. Though community members widely respected Fiona's grandfather and praised him as a prominent religious leader, he was a different person in private. He emotionally and physically abused Fiona's mother, his only child. As a result, Fiona's mom struggled with depression throughout her life.

Over the years, Fiona has often spoken about her mom's struggle with depression and has always supported my mental health advocacy work. In fact, she co-authored the legislation that created the California Office of Suicide Prevention. Fiona, I know from personal experience, champions what she believes in and makes the change she wants to see.

In 2009, Fiona watched a documentary by filmmaker Olivia Klaus called *Sin by Silence*, which featured the life of Brenda Clubine. Brenda had served twenty-six years in prison and dedicated her new life to helping her "sisters" still in prison. The documentary depicted the dire circumstances faced by Brenda and other women who were convicted of life without parole for killing their abusers—including Rosemary Dyer, who had developed many serious health ailments during her twenty-four years in prison and had given up all hopes of ever being released. Compelled to act on behalf of the women still trapped by the injustice of the system, Fiona visited Rosemary and others in state prison to see and hear firsthand from the women who were invisible to the outside world.

Inspired by her new friendship with Brenda Clubine, in 2012, Fiona introduced Assembly Bills (AB) 1593 and 593, also known as the "Sin by Silence" bills, named after the documentary that prompted the effort. These two bills allowed abused women serving life without parole to have their cases reviewed by the State Board of Parole Hearings. AB 593 sought to clarify the government Penal Code 1473.5 to include domestic violence victims like Rosemary, who were denied their writ of habeas corpus due to limited expert testimony evidence. AB 1593 sought to provide victims of domestic violence who suffered Intimate Partner Battering (IPB) a chance to present their evidence effectively during the parole process. Governor Jerry Brown signed both bills into law on September 30, 2012, ensuring freedom for over seven thousand domestic violence survivors serving time in California prisons.

As a result of Fiona's groundbreaking legislation, women are still being released from prison today.

Fiona organized a letter-writing campaign for Rosemary, urging the governor to commute Rosemary Dyer's sentence. In 2020, after a review by the parole board, Governor Gavin Newsom commuted Rosemary's sentence. She was released in April of that year.

Women legislators—like Fiona—make a difference in the issues they prioritize and the bills they sponsor. Published in the *Journal of Politics*, Kathlene Lyn wrote an article titled, "Alternative View of Crime: Legislative Policymaking in Gendered Terms," explaining that, "Because they are more concerned with context and environmental factors when delivering on crime and punishment, women state assemblymembers are more likely than men to advocate for rehabilitation programs and less likely than men to punitive policies."

Today, Fiona is still involved in helping women like Rosemary. She continued her domestic violence victim advocacy work long after being termed out of the state assembly. She also is still making fundraising calls for Home Free, a nonprofit that has helped women released from prison secure permanent housing.

And when Rosemary was finally released from prison in 2020—thirty-three and a half years after her initial incarceration—Fiona drove over six hours to the California Women's Institution in Chino to pick her up. After spending three decades in prison, Rosemary's family and friends weren't around; she had no place to go. Fiona helped Rosemary secure housing and the resources she needed to start living her life at the age of sixty-seven. "If it weren't for Fiona," Rosemary told me during my visit to her Treasure Island home, "I would live in a cardboard box somewhere."

Representation matters. Without it, vulnerable people slip through the cracks in the system and never see the freedom or change they deserve. Without it, we miss out on vital perspectives and vital champions, like Fiona, who can help create the equitable world our democracy promises.

WOMEN LEGISLATORS WORK FOR WOMEN

Michele Swers, a professor of American Government in the Department of Government at Georgetown University, has authored two books on women and representation in Congress.[20] In an interview with the Institute for Women's Policy Research, Michele noted that her interest in women in politics began when her grandmother shared stories about Eleanor Roosevelt and gave her a book about first ladies.[21]

Michele Swers's research findings, spanning over two decades, focus on women's impact on policymaking and how women in Congress have leveraged their position to advance gender-specific policy goals. A key finding is that women legislators are more likely to introduce legislation that impacts women and children. For example, women in Congress advocated for landmark legislation such as the Violence Against Women Act and the Lilly Ledbetter

Fair Pay Act, demonstrating a clear connection between women's representation in Congress and increased policy achievements for women's rights issues.

When we look at the legacy of Patricia Schroeder, a former legislator who championed gender equality, we can clearly see the impact one female legislator can make. Patricia engineered the Family and Medical Leave Act of 1993, which guarantees women and men up to twelve weeks of unpaid leave to care for a family member. She also helped pass legislation which prohibits employers from discriminating against pregnant women in employment.

Patricia Schroeder was also a pilot and a Harvard lawyer who worked to improve the lives of military personnel. She suggested that women be allowed to fly combat missions. As a result, Defense Secretary Les Aspin ordered women to do so, and in 1995, the first woman fighter pilot was flying in combat. When Patricia became the first woman to serve on the Arms Services Committee in Congress, her critics asked how she was able to raise two children as a mom and work as a lawmaker.

Women's rights issues reach far beyond increased protection for victims of domestic violence, spanning the realms of public health and the economy. For example, one of the sixty precedent-setting bills that Fiona authored—which were signed into law by two different governors—banned toxic chemicals, known as phthalates, in baby products. This state legislation became a model for the federal legislation that US Senator Dianne Feinstein ultimately authored in 2008.

However, the work of advocating for gender equality continues to this day. Twenty-eight years ago, a champion for women's rights, then-Assemblywoman Jackie Speier authored the Gender Tax Repeal Act of 1995, which prohibited price differentials for goods that are similar. In 2022, my own state assemblywoman, Rebecca Bauer-Kahan, accomplished important anti-discrimination legislation. She expanded the Gender Repeal Tax Act to address the so-called "pink tax," where products marketed to women cost more than identical products marketed to men. Thanks to AB 1287, California businesses are no longer allowed to charge a higher price on products marketed for women.

In a related statement, Rebecca said, "Paying a financial cost for being a woman is unjust and only adds to the gender wage and wealth gaps. This type of arbitrary gendered pricing has no place in California. It's past time to ensure price equality."

Holly Martinez, executive director of the California Commission on the Status of Women and Girls, also stated, "Women make up as much as 85 percent of consumer purchases in the United States, and the Pink Tax represents $1,300 that can't go into a women's retirement fund, toward home ownership, toward her education, or to feed her family."

Would these bills have been passed without women participating in the legislative process? Taking pride in being a female in government and recognizing the importance of their presence, these women have prioritized legislative issues through a female lens, using their personal life experiences to impact public policy matters. Without these women, many of these important gender equality perspectives and protections would not be possible.

WHY REPRESENTATION MATTERS

Representation is important for more than gender equity; it also matters when it comes to other underrepresented groups. I learned this lesson early in my career, when I was working as an advocate for Asian American health.

In the 1990s, Vice President Al Gore championed a tobacco cessation campaign. Its mission was to prevent children from smoking, including initiatives such as reducing tobacco marketing to teens and restricting the accessibility of cigarettes. The Centers for Disease Control and Prevention (CDC) pledged massive support for implementing these national tobacco intervention programs, including running a comprehensive study on Americans' tobacco use in 1994.

The study found that only 14 percent of Asian Americans were smokers, the lowest among all racial groups.[22] But given my personal experience in the Asian community, I knew that this data was not accurate. I also knew, since studies such as this dictated funding for national educational and health programs, that Asian Americans would miss out on such resources if it were believed they were not an at-risk group.

Upon further investigation, I discovered that the CDC's survey had been conducted in English, only by phone, and used a small sample size. So, I raised $75,000 and partnered with the American Cancer Society to create our own survey. We used the same questions the CDC study used but translated them into Korean and Vietnamese, two of the most common languages spoken by Asian Americans. This time, the sample size and selection were sufficiently representative of the Asian population, and we hired professional, bilingual interviewers to conduct the surveys in each respondent's preferred language. Eighty-nine percent of the surveyed Vietnamese and 82 percent of the Koreans asked to take the study in their native language, not English.

As I expected, the results were substantially different from the CDC studies. For example, our survey found that 34 percent of Vietnamese and 31 percent of Korean American men smoked, compared to the CDC's study, which found that 20 percent of the same demographic smoked. Even more interesting was the finding that Asian American men smoked more than Caucasian men, which was a reported 20 percent.

And there was not just a smoking problem in the Asian American community. The results of the survey revealed that awareness and education were also severely lacking. Roughly 20 percent of those surveyed said they were unaware of the deadly effects of smoking. 34 percent of Vietnamese respondents said they didn't know tobacco was addictive.

In 1996, I began traveling to Washington, DC, to lobby Congress for better Asian American data collection. The representative for

California's eighth district, Rep. Nancy Pelosi, supported the effort by starting a letter-writing campaign, urging Congress to support the inclusion of Asians and Pacific Islanders in data collection efforts by the federal government, including the CDC. Anna Eshoo, Patsy Mink, and several other female legislators supported the action and even met with me one-on-one to discuss our concerns and carry our message to Congress.

The non-representative data collection methods used by the CDC failed to identify a significant health epidemic in the Asian community. Fortunately, the CDC quickly learned from its harmful oversight, and in 1998, I launched an entirely new study in partnership with CDC's Office on Smoking. This time around, the study focused on the age at which Asian Americans began smoking, which we found by interviewing Asian youth between the ages of thirteen and eighteen at venues like cultural youth clubs and ethnic language schools.

Through my non-profit organization's efforts and partnerships, we built a comprehensive and accurate picture of smoking among Asian American communities and ensured adequate allocation of public resources to education and health programs. Without representation, the distribution of these valuable resources would have skipped over the Asian community, and the genuine issue of smoking amongst Asian Americans would have gone entirely unaddressed. This is precisely why representation matters.

On June 7, 1999, a coalition of other Asian American health advocates, including Nancy Pelosi, Anna Eshoo, and I witnessed President Clinton's signing of Executive Order 13125, which established the first White House Initiative on Asian Americans and Pacific Islanders. This executive order mandated that all federal government programs include Asian Americans in their supporting research efforts and data collection.

Standing a few feet from President Clinton in the Oval Office was a surreal moment. By taking action and advocating for policy changes, I championed the inclusion of Asian Americans in the equitable distribution of public funds. This effort marked significant strides toward equality in areas such as health, housing, employment, and other programs.

This was representation, and I was hooked.

FEMALE-MAJORITY STATE LEGISLATURE

It can be easy to ignore just how powerful and potent representation is, but it would be a mistake to do so. Putting women in positions of power changes the dynamics of what the state becomes because women are more likely to draw attention to those who are marginalized or side-lined—and what we draw attention to is what we change.

In December 2018, Nevada's legislature became the first to hold a female majority, and in the next election in 2020, even more women were elected to the legislature. As of the November 2022 election cycle, Nevada is the state with the most significant number of women in its legislature, with an increase from 52 percent female legislators in 2019 to 59 percent in 2022.[23] In Nevada, both the Senate Republican Minority Leader and the Senate Democratic Majority Leader are women.

"What is it like to work in a female majority legislature?" I asked Senator Dallas Harris, who was appointed to the Nevada State Senate seat in District 11 in December 2018. "Do you think the work and culture of a female majority legislature are different from a male majority legislature?"

"Absolutely!" Dallas responded. She said that she wouldn't be here without trailblazers like State Senator Pat Spearman, the first openly lesbian and African American member serving in the Nevada State Legislature. She emphasized the significance of the presence of other women in the legislature, and that personal experiences and identities influence their legislative priorities.

Dallas also described how the Nevada women's caucus channeled their passion to addressing issues that affect women. "As of January 2020, the state of Nevada requires all employers with fifty or more employees to provide at least forty hours of paid leave annually to its workers." In addition to the family paid leave policy, Nevada passed legislation that requires equal pay for equal work, as well as legislation that requires companies to pay workers for lost wages if they intentionally engage in gender pay discrimination. As a former public interest attorney, Dallas sees herself as a voice for those groups whom lobbyists do not represent: the poor.

Nevada legislators recently enacted legislation called the Trust Nevada Women Act, decriminalizing certain restrictions related to abortion. Another successful Nevada legislation focused on firefighters who develop breast, uterine, and ovarian cancer because of work-related exposure to toxic contaminants.

Nevada is one of the few states to recognize women's cancer types as an occupational disease. In an interview with BBC News, Senate Majority Leader Nicole Cannizzaro explained the need for this bill. "It had never been something that people thought of—but we have a lot of women serving as firefighters now," she said. "They were exposed to the same chemicals—often cancerous—but were not covered for the same type of work as their [male] counterparts."[24] As a result of this legislation, these women firefighters can now receive compensation for their work injuries.

Studies show that female legislators claim their experiences as women give them critically different perspectives from their male counterparts, motivating them to address public policy issues that affect the most vulnerable and underrepresented communities. Electing more women has clearly changed how the government works for its people.

PART II

BARRIERS

CHAPTER 4

THE WAY WE SEE OURSELVES

"No country can ever truly flourish if it stifles
the potential of its women and deprives itself of the
contributions of half its citizens."
—MICHELLE OBAMA

When I decided to run for office, it wasn't because someone had encouraged me; rather, I'd seen many brilliant role models and was inspired by the change I could make. So once I had made the decision, I reached out to my local Democratic Party Chairwoman for advice and guidance. She suggested we meet at the San Francisco Embarcadero Center coffee place close to her work.

During the meeting, I shared with her my enthusiasm for and commitment to public service, as well as my passion for mental health services. She seemed hesitant, asking me, "Have you thought about running for the local hospital board first?" She was concerned that I wasn't ready for elected office because I hadn't already served in a local government position.

The question took me aback. I asked, "Are you asking the same question to my male opponent, who never ran for City Council or the board of directors for a local hospital?" She didn't reply.

That meeting wasn't the first discouragement I'd faced. Many of those serving in local government had also encouraged me not to run, claiming previous campaign experience was necessary to win.

But I knew I was qualified by all official standards. I had endorsements from Tipper Gore, Congresswoman Anna Eshoo, then-San Francisco District Attorney Kamala Harris, numerous leaders in healthcare, Congress, and the women's rights community. I had years of experience running healthcare advocacy and public policy programs and high-profile work like Proposition 63. My opponent, a man who had served as the county fire chief, had never run for office either. Yet, somehow, no one challenged his readiness to run for state assembly. He was automatically qualified.

I did not heed the doubters' advice, and I ran anyway. But the local County Democratic Party Chair's discouraging words still haunt me to this day. No matter how confident you are, it is tough to internalize that you are still qualified when people start doubting your abilities. Even though recent decades have improved women's rights and opportunities, our society is still used to seeing men in positions of power far more often than women.

The message conveyed to today's generation of young women is that they, too, can be leaders. It's an important message and a great start to an essential cultural shift, but while the message is strong and opportunities for women are theoretically available, we have limited authentic engagement and gender parity in most areas of society, including our government.

The reason for this delay between the objective and the result is simple: A new narrative, combined with a few decades of affirmative action, cannot immediately erase centuries of gender bias and discrimination. The Nineteenth Amendment and the Women's Movement permitted us to participate in our country's political process and economy, but full engagement and representation require a comprehensive cultural shift. And that takes time.

When I interviewed Amanda Hunter, executive director of the Barbara Lee Family Foundation, for this book, she described the organization's most recent focus group research. When participants were asked to picture a governor, an overwhelming majority said they envisioned a man. This phenomenon is a version of what's commonly known as "unconscious bias." The Barbara Lee Family Foundation has given this specific version of unconscious bias a name: the imagination barrier. It is what keeps voters from envisioning women and women of color in elected offices that for centuries have been held by white men.[25] We cannot imagine seeing a different kind of person doing these jobs.

Just as our "good girl" training will take generations to undo, so will this imagination barrier. Unfortunately, it's much more complicated than assuming younger people will exhibit less unconscious gender and racial bias. In her eloquent article published by the BBC, writer Christine Ro pointed out that the Reykjavik Index Survey showed that around the world, young men were unlikely to support women in power.[26] Although the perception of the younger generation of men may appear more progressive than the older generation of men, younger men think that women are already represented in positions of power in government. Could it be that they imagine the best leaders to be men, and so when some leaders are women, young men feel that women are overrepresented in government?

While we've gotten closer to a state of gender parity, we are not there yet. Significant cultural shifts like women's role in our society require policy and behavioral change. We've made strides on the former, but the latter is much more nuanced and takes more time to complete.

Despite our best efforts to tear them down, cultural barriers keep women from stepping into public office. These cultural barriers are the qualification gap, the ambition gap, and likability double standards.

THE QUALIFICATION GAP: EXTERNAL AND SELF-IMPOSED

In a research study titled *Men Rule: The Continued Under-Representation of Women in U.S. Politics*, Jennifer Lawless and Richard Fox found that men were almost 60 percent more likely than women to assess themselves as "very qualified" to run for office. Women, meanwhile, were more than twice as likely as men to rate themselves as "not at all qualified." In addition, most male respondents who said they were not qualified also said they would still consider running.[27] A similar phenomenon happens in the corporate world, where men apply for positions when they meet just 60 percent of the required qualifications; in contrast, women only apply for the same position if they meet 100 percent of the required qualifications.[28]

The standard explanation for this gap is that women lack confidence and are reluctant to pursue a position they are unsure they can adequately perform. But if we dig deeper, it becomes apparent that this "confidence" explanation is either too simplistic or entirely inaccurate.

When a job description states a set of required qualifications and a woman does not meet each item, she will usually not apply. She knows that the purpose of the listed requirements is to weed out those who are unqualified, even if that means her. She is a "good girl" by following the rules and not giving herself special treatment or over-evaluating her worth. On the other hand, men often believe that certain exceptions will be made for them and that they have a chance at consideration even if they do not meet every listed requirement.

In fact, we find that people's gendered beliefs about their qualifications are upheld by their experiences. Even if a man meets only 60 percent of the required qualifications at the interview table, the evaluator often makes an exception. Whether it's his personality traits, demonstrated ambition or ongoing pursuits of additional degrees or certifications, the man's *potential* is given heavy consideration in addition to his existing qualifications.

Women, on the other hand, are not granted such leeway. Because of the imagination barrier, it's harder for the evaluator to consider the potential of a woman who has the same qualifications as a man. This is true of a manager evaluating prospects for a job and voters evaluating candidates for office.

After a handful of attempted progressive career moves—perhaps some successful and some unsuccessful—women quickly learn this reality. We realize that we are expected to meet all stated requirements if we want to be considered for a role, especially if we are being evaluated against an equally qualified man. It's not that we lack the confidence to apply ourselves even if we don't meet all the qualifications; it's that we've repeatedly seen that we are unfairly held to a higher standard than our male counterparts.

There is no better example of this inequity than the political career of Hillary Clinton. Not only has Hillary been scrutinized more for her appearance and mannerisms than any male politician, but her experience and competence have continuously been held to much higher standards. For example, in 2008, despite having a law degree from Yale Law School, decades of experience as a community activist, several terms as a US senator, and in spite of the fact that she is a highly recognizable public figure, Hillary lost her bid for the Democratic presidential nomination to a then little-known male senator from Illinois.

In 2016, when Hillary Clinton again ran for president (this time with the title "Secretary of State" added to her resume), she successfully secured the Democratic nomination. She was more than qualified for the job. Her competition, Republican candidate Donald Trump, had zero political experience. However, even though he had never held a single public office position, he had an abundance of confidence and genuinely believed he was qualified to be President of the United States.

Hillary's political rivals argued that she had taken numerous missteps in her previous leadership roles, and they concocted scandals to diminish her integrity. But the weakest, most troubling argument was that she wasn't qualified to be president when compared to someone like Donald Trump. With all the qualifications in the world, running against someone with none, Hillary Clinton lost the election. This result made it abundantly clear that women running for public office are held to a different—nearly impossible—standard.

Unfortunately, Hillary Clinton's tumultuous presidential pursuits played out on the public stage in front of an entirely new generation of American women. As a result, millions of women now think, "If Hillary Clinton isn't recognized as a competent leader, how could I ever be?" According to the study, *Men Rule*, 84 percent of women felt that Hillary Clinton experienced gender bias in the 2008 election, a perception that will undoubtedly dissuade other women from similarly following in her footsteps.

While confidence may be a hurdle for some women attempting to advance in their careers, it is not the primary reason women are so underrepresented in corporate leadership roles, entrepreneurship, and government. Qualified, competent women know what we are capable of. We are fully aware of how well we could perform in various positions of power. However, through years of attempts at progression—and having front-row seats to atrocities like Hillary Clinton's career—we have learned that the evaluation process is an uphill battle, one that still largely favors men. Therefore, women who would otherwise gladly take on a leadership role at their company or run for public office end up not bothering.

During my interview with renowned pollster and political strategist Celinda Lake, Celinda described the phenomenon of compounding perceptions: "Democrats tend to be weak on crime; women tend to be weak on crime. So if you're a woman and a Democrat, voters assume you are weak on crime." Celinda then described how the 2022 election cycle was an interesting time for women candidates, particularly because the two dominant issues were the economy and crime. "Voters don't think women are as strong on the economy. Confidence matters as much as competence. But gender stereotypes held by voters may disadvantage women candidates. Even when women are self-assured about their qualifications, women candidates must deal with voters who often use gender stereotypes to evaluate political candidates."

Still, there is something even more troubling about women's qualifications being assessed differently than men's qualifications. The most extraordinary injustice takes place when a woman undervalues *herself*. What happens when we evaluate ourselves as 60 percent qualified when we are 100 percent qualified? This self-doubt, this underestimation of our qualifications, is among the most significant barriers keeping women from elected office.

The number one reason women give for not getting involved in politics is that they don't have the right experience. But according to the US Constitution, there are only three requirements to become President of the United States: You must be at least thirty-five years old, you must have been born in the United States or its territories, and you must have lived in the United States for at least fourteen years. The requirements for other offices are equally simple.

In addition to these basic qualifications, to have a successful campaign, you must also have leadership experience in community activism or with a nonprofit or government organization. Having a network of friends, colleagues, and supporters also helps. And, of course, you need a solid campaign team with a winning strategy.

Is running for public office more nuanced than this? Of course. Does the current system favor the wealthy and well-connected? Absolutely. But all the other perceived "requirements," such as wealth, an Ivy League education, or even masculine traits are false barriers. They have been concocted by those who've traditionally held power (men) and are afraid of losing it to those who are fully qualified and possibly even better leaders (women).

Dr. Lisa Reynolds, a physician of pediatrics and Oregon state legislator, told me about the moment she realized she was just as qualified to serve in public office as anyone else. "Through my involvement with Moms Demand Action, I had been lobbying state legislators in Salem quite a lot when it hit me. I realized that while these state representatives are smart people, I was just as smart and capable as them. I could do what they were doing."

Dr. Reynolds raises another important point about our "good girl" upbringing with this observation. Young girls are raised to have so much respect for authority that women often end up with an over-inflated perception of those who serve in public office. But in reality, public officials are human, just like the rest of us.

Former California Assemblywoman Sunny Mojonnier echoed Dr. Reynolds's realization when she explained one of the most important lessons she learned during her forty-year career. "I learned that running for office is something that anybody who passionately believes in an issue, a business, or a necessary piece of legislation can do. Yes, there are lawyers. I served with doctors, lawyers, dentists, previous staff members, and nurses, some Ivy League-educated and some not, because they all put themselves forward and said 'I could do this.' So, I learned that any one of us can do this."

When she first began campaigning for her first election in December 2019, Dr. Reynolds realized she had a unique qualification that could set her apart from her opponents: she was a doctor.

"I was going door-to-door, and when I mentioned I'm a doctor, people would ask me what kind. When I answered that I was a pediatrician, they had a positive association with me. People automatically trust physicians because they know we are smart, hard-working, and have others' interests at heart."

Dr. Reynolds explained to me how her experience as a doctor also made her a very effective politician. "In the exam room, I'm used to meeting all kinds of people and facing serious problems with strangers. I'm very comfortable making a connection with people." She also pointed out how her many years in medical school and practicing medicine prepared her well for the grueling work and long hours.

Like men, women candidates can find success by identifying and leveraging their unique qualifications. This strategy serves to differentiate candidates, and women's qualifications are often just as distinct as those of their male opponents.

THE AMBITION GAP

It is widely known that girls take less interest in the fields of science, technology, engineering, and math (STEM) than their male peers. Any interest they do show is often unencouraged, and so their interest diminishes further as they get older. It is also widely recognized that we need educated, competent women represented in these disciplines to ensure equality and diversity of thought. Therefore, over recent decades, schools, universities, institutions, and even entire industries have joined forces to put programs in place to foster girls' interest and participation in STEM.

Girls' interest in politics follows a similar pattern to that of STEM. At an early age, girls express interest in a career in government at a much lower rate than boys, and the gap widens over time. In a 2013 study titled *Girls Just Wanna Not Run* by the American University School of Public Affairs, male and female college students were surveyed about their involvement and interest in politics. On every single measure, the men's responses were significantly higher than the women's, including having held positions in student government, been involved in College Democrats or Republicans organizations, taking a political science or government class, and frequently discussing politics and current events with friends.[29] This lack of interest translates into an ambition gap: fewer women have the ambition to become politicians than men do.

One significant reason girls possess less interest in politics than boys is because of the imagination barrier. If you—and the people around you—cannot imagine someone like you doing a job, it's much less likely for you to develop an interest in that career. The imagination barrier results in a range of factors that contribute to women having less interest than men in running for political office; the authors of *Girls Just Wanna Not Run* identify five of them:[30]

1. Young men are more likely than young women to be socialized by their parents to think about politics as a career path.

2. From their school experiences to their peer associations to their media habits, young women tend to be exposed to less political information and discussion than do young men.

3. Young men are more likely than young women to have played organized sports and care about winning.

4. Young women are less likely than young men to receive encouragement to run for office—from anyone.

5. Young women are less likely than young men to think they will be qualified to run for office, even once they are established in their careers.

These deeply ingrained cultural factors make it difficult for women to drum up the desire to run for political office at the rate needed to reach gender parity.

Items one through three represent how boys and girls are treated differently in our culture, which are similar to the reasons for girls' lack of interest in STEM. Like the STEM programs of recent decades, these cultural barriers require purposeful and ongoing programs to give girls more exposure to politics, competition, and opportunities in government. Item number four describes the qualification gap discussed earlier. Lastly, item number five reveals an essential opportunity: People who can see beyond the imagination barrier can help women picture themselves as politicians.

Research indicates that competent women will run for office—and win—if encouraged to do so. A study by the Center for American Women in Politics (CAWP) discovered that 53 percent of female state representatives answered that they "had not seriously thought about running until someone else suggested it." In contrast, only 28 percent of male representatives answered this way. Forty-three percent of the male state representatives answered, "It was entirely my idea to run," whereas only 26 percent of women responded this way.[31]

There are two high-level reasons why people run for public office. One reason is that they desire to hold a leadership position. Sometimes, there is a particular office which they seek for the title and gravitas. Sometimes, any part of the power will do. But the goal is the position itself, not the work that comes with it.

This also happens in the private sector, where ambitious professionals seek to climb the corporate ladder no matter the cost. These individuals don't care about what products their company makes or how their work impacts others. They seek a particular title or level of power—that corner office.

In 1963, a sixteen-year-old high school student named Bill Clinton had the opportunity to shake hands with President John F. Kennedy as a participant in the American Legion program Boys Nation (for now, let's ignore the name and the fact that no girls participated in this program). It was a turning point in the impressionable teenager's life, as his peers later recounted how Clinton spent the bus ride back to the dormitories claiming that one day, he would have Kennedy's job. Starstruck and having caught a glimpse of what it's like to be someone in a position of power, Clinton was attracted to the vision of himself in that position.

People also run for political office because they care deeply about an issue and are compelled to do something about it. They see political office as their way to affect change in a certain way that is important to them. These individuals typically never planned to run for public office and, unlike Bill Clinton, did not daydream as teenagers of one day having a powerful title.

For example, as a mother of two children, the repeated atrocities of school gun violence hit Dr. Lisa Reynolds close to home, so she became involved with an organization called Moms Demand Action. Through her work lobbying at the state capitol, Dr. Reynolds realized that she could do even more for the safety of her children and all children by serving in public office. She decided to run for state legislature in the November 2020 election.

Dr. Reynolds's interest in public office only increased when the COVID-19 pandemic hit early on in her campaign. She was featured in a May 9, 2020, article in *The New York Times* that examined the number of physicians running for office in reaction to the government's COVID-19 response. Dr. Reynolds said throughout the pandemic, "If I were a legislator I would be camping outside the governor's office saying I don't think we're moving fast enough on this."[32]

Dr. Reynolds is not the only example of passionate change. While Dr. Jean Fuller spent her entire career working for the children of California's Central Valley, upon her retirement as Superintendent of the Bakersfield City School District, Dr. Fuller decided to run for state assembly. She felt called to raise awareness of the many issues faced by educators in the public school system. She was appalled by problems like lengthy delays in school funding, which had dire consequences for teachers, students, and staff.

"I had a personal mission," Dr. Fuller told me. "Whether or not I won the election, I felt compelled to make the issues known and do whatever I could to improve things."

Men tend to run for office because they seek a leadership position; women, on the other hand, tend to run because of an issue they care about deeply, such as those related to children and families. Through our advocacy experience, we realize we can do more by holding public office. This is precisely what happened with Dr. Reynolds and Dr. Fuller, and it's what happened to me after I began advocating for mental health and Asian American women.

Neither reason for running for office is "wrong," but this difference explains why so many more boys than girls express interest in politics. It is rare for children—boys or girls—to have political issues they feel passionately about and subsequent plans to run for office to advocate for these issues. But young boys might know at an early age that when they grow up, they want to be in a position of power.

This difference in motivation also explains why it is so hard to recruit women to run for office. People who already have an innate desire to obtain a position of power (more often men than women) don't need to be recruited. But intelligent, competent people who do not have an innate desire to obtain a position of power require encouragement, even once they have a cause they are passionate about.

Most successful female politicians I speak with say that someone encouraged them—or at least planted the seed of the idea for them—to run for political office. This is an encouraging solution to the cultural issue of girls not being raised thinking about a career in politics. Women can still become interested in running for office with the encouragement of others.

But even after encouragement, we face another barrier: recruiting political candidates. We want authentic, qualified people to be the ones who lead us, but many genuine, well-meaning people often self-select out of running for office because they don't want to deal with politics. Since they have no intrinsic motivation to obtain a position of power, even if they feel passionate about an issue, they might not be willing to face the realities of what it takes to run and serve.

Overall, successful recruitment is a tough task to accomplish and the necessary encouragement is not happening, at least not at the rate needed to drive change. Several political party leaders interviewed for this book found that there was no concerted effort to recruit women candidates, particularly women of color candidates. However, the same leaders claimed no gender bias and stated that all viable candidates were welcome.

This unenthusiastic attitude and the misguided assumption that all qualified individuals will magically step forward and run is entirely naive. To overcome inequality, those in positions of power and influence must do their part to proactively support the underrepresented. When the day comes that women make up at least half of all legislative and executive offices in this country, then and only then can party leaders sit back and say, "May the best man (or woman) win." Until then, proactive recruitment of women is necessary.

Yet, even when there is a distinct focus on recruiting competent women, many resist running for public office. Campaigns mean spending less time with family, as the candidate must work to solicit contributions, deal with party officials, go door-to-door, manage the press, and respond to criticism, and deal with negative campaigning. Entering the electoral arena requires courage. It demands full commitment to putting yourself in front of the public, which can be scary. Unfortunately, according to the *Men Rule* study, women tend to be less competitive and more risk averse than their male counterparts.[33]

Why is that? One reason could be because women tend to make decisions based on the needs of their family and, particularly, their children. Often, women don't think of running as a viable option even when they are qualified. So, when I had the chance to interview former Fremont, California city councilwoman Sue Chan, I desperately wanted to ask her why she never ran for state legislative office. Sue chose not to run despite impressive recruitment efforts from the California Dental Association and numerous high-profile elected officials.

"My work ethic is that if I commit to doing something, I need to be sure I can do it fully at one hundred percent," Sue explained. "After weighing the personal sacrifices that would be required to serve in Sacramento, I didn't believe I could make that level of commitment. And I didn't want to occupy a seat for a four-year term only to decide I couldn't continue." Sue went on to describe how much she loathed the logistics of campaigning, fundraising, public events, and commuting to Sacramento. "If I could do the work without all that, I would do it in a heartbeat."

Many women like Sue, who believe themselves qualified and have the ambition to run, still decide against running because they find the entire campaign process unappealing. On the public stage, you can expect to be scrutinized for everything from your appearance to your beliefs to your family; the media and public have no problem asking candidates direct questions about their personal lives because people believe they are entitled to private information about the lives of public servants. Such an invasion of privacy takes a mental and emotional toll, and this adjustment can be hard, especially for women, who undoubtedly receive much more scrutiny than men.

Even worse than a lack of recruitment, many qualified women are *discouraged* from running. CAWP research shows that about one-third of women legislators say someone—often an officeholder or political party official—tried to prevent them from running , just as I experienced. [34] This unnecessary discouragement of women moves us backward rather than forwards and serves to increase the ambition gap.

Women are discouraged from running for all sorts of reasons. Perhaps the party leader who discouraged me thought I couldn't win without more campaign experience, or perhaps she felt that there were limited opportunities for women and minorities and therefore felt threatened by an up-and-coming candidate in the same demographic. Other candidates may be held to impossibly high standards and told not to run.

For example, in 2022, the local Democratic party refused to consider endorsing an Asian woman legislative candidate in the San Francisco Bay Area because she held some conservative views. She became a Democrat over twenty years ago, when she realized her stance on key issues was more liberal than conservative, but her beginnings as a Republican disqualified her in the eyes of the party. But the same local Democratic party expressed public appreciation when a local county supervisor, a white male, also changed his party affiliation from Republican to Democrat. The same local Democratic party welcomed him with open arms, even holding a press conference to thank him for switching his political affiliation. This blatant gender-based denunciation is a gross disservice to women.

Most women politicians who have won their campaign for the state legislature had party support.[35] Still, party leaders must consciously hold all candidates to the same standards, regardless of gender and race. They must take a close look at themselves and remove their unconscious biases. Both Democratic and Republican party leaders must take a proactive approach to seeking out and encouraging competent women at all levels of legislative and executive government, and do more to close the ambition gap.

Sunny Mojonnier once pointed out to me that Republican women tend to have the reputation that they don't support women due to their position on a few specific female-focused issues. But more women in government is not a party issue; it is a citizen issue. We need more women—of all political affiliations—if we want to reach the gender parity Sunny and her friends began pursuing back in the eighties.

LIKABILITY DOUBLE STANDARDS

In her book, *The Likability Trap: How to Break Free and Succeed as You Are*, author Alicia Menendez says, "Studies have found that when the press talks about a woman candidate's looks, she becomes less likable. It doesn't matter whether the coverage is positive, negative, or neutral." Menendez goes on to explain that, "even if the press discusses a man's appearance (which is very rare since there isn't much variation in style amongst male politicians), such coverage does not have the same impact on a man as it does on a woman."

It's not just a woman's appearance that gets much more attention than it should. Our mannerisms and behavioral traits are often the focus of women politicians. With our "good girl" upbringing, women are not encouraged to be strong and assertive.

In Korean culture, the behaviors required to run for and serve in public office do not come naturally for women. Our society values more masculine style leadership, and we are often told we do not have what it takes to lead because of our more feminine personality traits. As a young girl, I was told to be modest; I should undervalue my skills and accomplishments and never exhibit self-promotion. As I got older, I often worried about coming across as too strong, too opinionated, or taking too much credit.

Because of cultural factors like these, when a woman announces her candidacy for public office, people often view her with distrust, and her motivations for running are questioned. No matter what we do, we are often penalized for being ambitious, and this puts us at a significant disadvantage.

In *The Likability Trap*, Menendez explains again: "While male candidates may struggle with likeability, research shows that voters will support a male candidate even if they don't like him, if they believe he is qualified for the job. Women candidates face a different test: to win, they need to be liked and perceived as competent. And while voters assume men are competent, women must prove they are."

In my interview with renowned pollster and political strategist Celinda Lake, I asked how women can address this issue of style over substance. How should we present ourselves to avoid the likability double standard? Her answer was two-fold: Candidates must exude confidence and demonstrate to voters that they are serious about serving in office. In other words, make sure that you "look the part."

"You have just forty-five seconds to make a first impression," Celinda said. "And if you don't get it right the first time, it's tough to recover." The good news, she added, is that voters have come a long way in what they consider acceptable for a candidate's style.

"It used to be the standard uniform: a classic suit and a simple haircut for men, which early female politicians adopted because they had no other option. But now, voters are accepting of more casual clothing and different hairstyles… There is more leeway in what is acceptable when a candidate presents themself as qualified."

When I spoke with Amanda Hunter of the Barbara Lee Family Foundation, she echoed Celinda's guidance, adding that while men like Bernie Sanders can be celebrated for a quirky disheveled look, women are not afforded the same leeway. "We cannot let anything be out of place. We must look completely put together but, at the same time, not *too* put together." At the same time, Amanda pointed out that voters want to know that a woman is serious and suited for the job; they don't want it to seem like she spends all her time at the hair and nail salon instead of developing policy.

"In our work," Amanda explained, "we've found it to be most effective when a woman finds a look that serves as her own 'uniform'—something that is uniquely her, professional, and authentic. You want people to remember the person, not her appearance." Amanda also agrees with Celinda's observation that voters have become more accepting of various styles. "In the eighties and nineties, when women first took a more prominent role in government, they had to fit into a mold made for men. But now, we've created our mold, which allows women to be our true selves instead of forcing us to be something we're not."

The double standards women face regarding their appearance and mannerisms exist at all levels of government. Yet they are the most extreme at executive levels of government, including the mayor and gubernatorial seats and, of course, presidential offices. In these very visible and powerful positions, the expectations are even higher, and double standards are more stringent.

In March 2022, Vice President Kamala Harris wore a brown suit during the State of the Union address. The color closely matched the leather chair that was behind her. While it may be true that the color and the boxy style of the Vice President's outfit did nothing to complement her, it certainly should not have been newsworthy. Yet social media went wild, calling for the fashion police and a makeover. A popular radio host compared the suit to a UPS uniform. President Biden's words were lost in a firestorm of tweets and other media attention that all focused on the Vice President's attire. This wasn't the first time, and it won't be the last time, that a female politician is judged on style over substance.

OVERCOMING BARRIERS

So, what can be done to break down these barriers that are so deeply ingrained in our culture and inside of ourselves? How do competent, capable women overcome the qualification gap, the ambition gap, and likability double standards? After all, there is no real reason for these barriers to exist; actual requirements did not create them. Instead, they were made from societal norms that have long been outgrown.

Recruitment is one of the few tools available to us now and can be used to throw into and disrupt the vicious cycle of the imagination barrier. If young girls don't take an interest in politics because they don't see females in these roles, then the next generation will not have any role models, and the cycle will continue.

It is up to our current leaders to break the wheel. They need to seek out and support women who don't just have the right experience and voting record but who have the political potential that is commonly recognized in men.

The good news is that we can overcome them by acknowledging them in others and in ourselves. Then, we can challenge these false barriers when we see and experience them.

When our qualifications are unfairly questioned—by others or by ourselves—we must fully articulate our actual qualifications and challenge those who undervalue them. When we feel intimidated by the political process or our ambition wanes, we must listen to the call to serve. When faced with infuriating double standards that require us to strike an impossible balance between our appearance, mannerisms, and likability, we must remain true to ourselves and present the woman who is competent, confident, and authentic.

CHAPTER 5

THE POLITICS OF MOTHERHOOD

"I have a brain and a uterus, and I use both."
—PATRICIA SCHROEDER

I n 2010, I was invited to participate in a panel of female leaders in government at the San Francisco Emerge candidates training. Emerge America is a national organization that brings together women of various backgrounds and offers training programs and resources to help women run for public office. Andrea Dew Steele, whom I met during my campaign for State Assembly, co-founded Emerge California in 2002. Later, in 2005, she founded Emerge America, which now has affiliates in over twenty-seven states. Andrea is a champion for Democratic women candidates and progressive causes.

During the question-and-answer session of the panel, one attendee raised the inevitable question, "Can I run for office even if I have young children?" The obvious answer was "Yes." After all, there is no official rule saying candidates cannot have young children. Men with young children have been serving in public office since the dawn of representative democracy.

Plus, motherhood serves as a unique qualification for public office. The various demands of motherhood often generate exceptional female leaders who fight hard for the health and welfare of children and families. Women tend to feel a collective responsibility for all children in their communities, and I've seen this countless times through the thoughtful policy- and decision-making of female leaders.

So, you *can* run for office if you have young children. But the woman in the audience at the Emerge training was asking a different question with a very different answer. I think she meant to ask, "Is it possible to run for office if you have extensive responsibilities managing a busy household and providing daily care for family members?"

This is a version of the classic question, "Is it possible to *have it all?*" which modern professional women have been asking for decades. Regardless of our profession, age, race, or even marital or parental status, this question haunts us all. It finds us in corporate boardrooms, in social circles, and yes, even in political offices. It asks whether or not it is possible to have a challenging, rewarding career while raising a happy, healthy family. It is a question unique to women because men do not struggle with the same demands when managing a career and a family simultaneously.

Can you run for office and manage a busy household? Maybe, but probably not. If you run for office, can you still put your family first whenever you need to? No, not likely. The myriad pressures women face around motherhood and family life highlight a range of different barriers to women serving in public office.

DIVISION OF DOMESTIC LABOR

Running for and serving in public office is highly demanding of one's time, as well as of one's mental and emotional strength. To be effective, it is unrealistic to expect to be home by five o'clock each night to make dinner and help your kids with homework. Likewise, it's difficult to be up with a sick toddler all night and present a powerful, compelling argument on the senate floor the following day.

However, it is possible to have a partner or a support system to manage most of these domestic responsibilities instead of attempting to handle them all alone. After all, for generations, men have been free to pursue careers in politics and business without worrying about who would cover their family's domestic responsibilities. Traditionally, most men in public office have a wife at home who manages all the duties. This allows the man the physical and mental bandwidth to focus on his campaigns, legislation, and networking without worrying about what's for dinner, how the kids are getting to soccer practice, or if the dog food is running low.

Despite women's political and economic advancement over recent decades, women and men continue to conform to the traditional division of labor at home. According to a study by AmericanProgress.org, "being the parent of a young child affects women's work hours—but not men's. Fathers and other men work the same total number of hours, but mothers of children under age 6 work fewer hours than men and women without small children." The study continues, "The majority of working mothers with young children return home from work only to engage in a second shift of unpaid household labor—and they do so at rates and with time investments that far exceed those of working fathers."[36]

The study, conducted from 2011 to 2016, showed that on an average weekday night, women perform 3.72 hours of household duties while men perform 2.83 hours. A roughly one-hour difference sounds small but can add up over time.[37]

Plus, the study did not consider other factors, such as what has recently become known as "the mental load"—the fact that women are the ones who mentally keep track of all the happenings of the family. Men willingly perform tasks as directed by their partners (the hours they spend each night, as noted in the study), but they don't keep track of what needs to be done. The time and energy women spend thinking about and keeping track of family matters has never been fully recognized or evaluated.

It is tough to dedicate oneself to a campaign at the level required by modern politics if you also carry the mental and physical workload of managing a household. And of course, when you're elected to public office, the workload will be just as challenging.

In recent years, more women have started relying on partners fully dedicated to domestic responsibilities or outsourcing the workload of managing a household to caregivers, personal cooks, and personal assistants. But in general, the unequal division of labor at home remains one of the most significant reasons so many women are uninterested in or unable to run for office. Their time is not their own, and they need more of it if they're going to dedicate any to public office.

According to the book, *A Seat at the Table: Congresswomen's Perspectives on Why Their Presence Matters* by Kelly Dittmar, Kira Sanbonmatsu, and Susan J. Carroll, just sixteen of the 108 women in the 114th Congress, including delegates, had children who were in high school or younger.[38] The book describes how, although women legislators today are better positioned to balance family obligations than they were in previous generations, women still struggle in ways that their male colleagues do not.

Even though women began having careers in the 1960s and 1970s, we continued carrying the bulk of household and family responsibilities. In recent years, men have started taking on a little more of the duties, but nowhere near to the point where we see stay-at-home dads supporting high-earning women as a regular occurrence in our society. The reasons for this are primarily cultural, but some are systemic, such as issues like the wage gap and the cost of childcare.

Why would a woman work when her male partner can make more money? Why would a woman work when her paycheck barely covers the cost of childcare?

The solution? Partners have to step up. For example, Sarah Palin had her bases covered at home when she ran for vice president of the United States alongside Senator John McCain in the 2008 presidential campaign. Her youngest child was born that same year, but her now ex-husband, Todd, took care of their Alaska home and five children while she was on the campaign trail.

Unfortunately, men who step up don't have it easy. As part of the McCain-Palin campaign's media circus, Todd Palin became the brunt of many jokes: the stay-at-home "dude," the man behind the woman, holding her purse at public appearances. He was emasculated for the unconventional role he played while his wife was off campaigning to become second in line for the presidency. This sent a loud message that not only are women bad moms if they hit the campaign trail and leave their children behind, but men aren't real men if they take care of their family while their wife pursues a political career.

Fourteen years later, we are closer to a place where the Palins's arrangement doesn't seem so unusual. I want to think their scenario would not be so heavily mocked and scrutinized today. After all, we now have our country's first male vice-presidential spouse, and for the first time, the needs of the female vice president will define his role. Many feminists around the country are thrilled seeing a white man step into a supporting role for the first Black and South Asian, female vice president—and actually enjoy doing it.

But in reality, these non-traditional partnerships are still far from the norm. According to Pew Research, the rate of stay-at-home fathers compared to stay-at-home mothers in the United States has remained almost the same since 1989. In 1989, 28 percent of mothers were unemployed at-home parents. In 2016, when the study was conducted, this rate was down just one point at 27 percent. By contrast, unemployed stay-at-home fathers were at 4 percent in 1989, and in 2016, this rate had increased slightly to just 7 percent.[39]

Of course, the 2020 COVID-19 pandemic drastically changed how working parents balance professional and family commitments. One potential candidate (who ultimately decided not to run for Congress due to family obligations) even asked me if remote voting would soon be allowed in Congress so that if he decided to run, he could fill his obligations while remaining in Oregon with his family.

While voting in person remains a requirement in 2023, the work environment is changing rapidly, in many ways for the better, as we incorporate more family-friendly and flexible work policies. As a part of this change, we will continue seeing more men step up to take on familial responsibilities, allowing more women to step into public office. After all, women have been doing so for men for centuries.

It's time for change.

THE *MOTHERHOOD* IMAGINATION BARRIER

In addition to the logistical challenges of caring for a household and a family while campaigning and serving, female candidates with families also face perception challenges. Just as our culture has a hard time picturing a "leader" as anything other than a white man, so do we have a hard time imagining a woman as anything other than a mother.

We singularly view women as caregivers. So, when a woman with children steps on the campaign trail, we immediately wonder who is looking after her children. She is seen as a horrible mother if she plans to have others—even Heaven forbid, the children's father—look after them. Or, if she intends to remain closely involved in her children's lives, she is deemed unfit for public office because she cannot possibly do the job while also caring for her children. But, of course, since our society does not see men as the primary caregivers, this issue is never a problem for men with young children who run for office. No reporters ask men, "Who's taking care of your children while you're on the campaign trail?"

In *A Seat at the Table*, Congresswoman Grace Meng described similar gender bias when she was criticized for bringing her young sons to events with her. The media commented that she hadn't been elected so that she could spend time with her children. On the other hand, a man being involved in his children's lives is viewed as noble. Instead of being criticized when his children attend campaign events, he is celebrated and regarded as a "family man."

Fortunately, this sexist cultural perception is slowly changing as younger generations of men take a more active role in their children's lives, and women step further into professional careers. As Second Gentleman Doug Emhoff proves, a man can be comfortable supporting a woman in a leadership role. Examples like this can break down the imagination barrier and change the way men view gender roles. For now out-of-date perceptions remain firmly in place—enough that this continues to create an additional challenge for women that men don't face.

THE *MOTHERHOOD* DOUBLE STANDARD

Even when a woman does *not* have children, she still has to contend with the public perception of women as mothers. Women face a double standard here: Their fitness to serve is challenged if they do have children, and their fitness to serve is challenged if they don't have children.

For example, during Cathleen Galgiani's assembly race, a member of her opponent's campaign team called her unmarried, childless, and lacking family values. Fortunately, Cathleen's keen campaign consultant used the blatant sexism to their advantage and called her opponent out for not denouncing the comments. But for Cathleen, the words did some damage.

"It hurt that after everything I'd done and accomplished, I was reduced to that part of who I am. And that it was construed in such a negative way that never would have been done to a man," Cathleen explained.

Because our culture views women as caregivers, if a woman has chosen a different path for herself, we tend to regard her with suspicion. "Why doesn't she have children? There must be an explanation…." This skepticism often translates to mistrust of a female candidate who does not have children.

Despite all her other qualifications and accomplishments, if a woman is missing the "motherhood" credential, it can hurt her chances in running for office. This is because voters might worry that she will be unable to truly understand family-related concerns. But, as you probably guessed, voters don't seem to have the same issues with a male candidate with no children.

PROTECTING OUR FAMILIES

The public scrutiny of one's hairstyle, pantsuit, or mannerisms is one thing, but the media going after one's spouse or children is an entirely different problem with much more severe consequences.

While it doesn't happen as much at the local level as at the state and federal level, invasion of privacy is a genuine issue that candidates face. Depending on the intensity of a particular race, opponents often use whatever information they can to tear one another down, and personal or family matters are fair play. As the (modified) saying goes, "All is fair in love and politics." Unfortunately, such ruthless tactics often lead to women stepping out of a race or deciding not to run in the first place.

In 2022, Giselle Hale, Mayor of Redwood City, California, decided to step down from her promising race for State Assembly. On the homepage of her website, Giselle explained her decision:

"I have never walked away from a fight, but I also know to choose my battles wisely. Coming from our broken childhoods, my husband and I know that having a stable family is a luxury, and putting my girls front and center of a battle that is not theirs to wage is not something I'm willing to do. So, today I'm choosing to fight for my family and wind down my campaign for the California State Assembly.

"While I could compartmentalize the lies and vicious attacks, focus on the issues, and keep driving, it was impossible for them not to internalize all of it. My five-year-old was regularly served one of my opponents' hate ads while watching a YouTube Kids' show, and my eight-year-old told me that a classmate brought a negative mailer to school.

"My experience isn't unique. You don't have to look hard in politics to find people willing to do or say anything to get elected. And you don't have to look far to see the people hurt by those campaigns. During my race, I lost count of the women who told me they would not run for office after watching the deluge of negative attacks. This cannot be the norm.

"I may be stepping back from my campaign for Assembly, but I will never step down from these tough fights. Change doesn't come to those who wait. It comes to those who fight for it. I intend to keep fighting—and I am asking you all to do the same."

It's worrisome enough that someone as genuine and passionate as Giselle felt she had to step back from a promising political career to protect her family. I respect her decision, but what I found even more worrisome was how Giselle described numerous women who claimed they would never run for office because of the treatment they saw Giselle receive.

Among the many stories she shared during our interview, this experience best described Giselle's decision to step down from her campaign for California State Assembly.

"A neighbor had stapled one of the hit pieces to his tree, a block from our home, like a wanted ad. It had my face contorted and a filter applied to make me look sinister. It was on the route my children took to the park. They later wrote 'Hale no' in chalk all over their sidewalk.

"Seeing people in our neighborhood do something like this was shocking to my kids, our family, and our neighbors. I learned later that these were parents with boys the same ages as my girls. What scared me at the time was realizing if people like them believed these lies, it was possible for worse, for one of the tens of thousands of people who received these ads to go a step further."

This invasion of privacy into families, especially its impact on children, is unacceptable and a disgrace to the American political process. It is also a barrier preventing many women from running for office.

Thanks to our "good girl" upbringing, women tend to be much more concerned about how our decisions and actions affect those around us, especially our families. We weigh the consequences of our decisions based on what we want for ourselves and how they might impact our broader familial ecosystem. In fact, the *Men Rule* study found that 30 percent of women reported that the threat of having less time for their family deterred them from running for office, while 21 percent of men said the same. 38 percent of women cited loss of privacy as a deterrent, whereas only 29 percent of men reported the same.[40]

This doesn't mean men don't care about their families. The difference is, historically speaking, even when faced with the personal challenges of a political campaign, men still run for office anyway.

But change is slowly happening. For example, in 2021, a state representative in Oregon chose not to seek re-election, citing his desire to focus on caring for his aging mother. That same year, he was being recruited to run for Congress by several high profile Democratic party leaders, so he reached out to members of Congress to see if he could serve while having two small children at home. He also called me asking if I could introduce him to members of Congress with children so he could better understand how they manage children and the demanding job. He then asked to speak with someone in Congress who could give him guidance on parenting while serving. But examples like his—men concerned with how a political career will impact their families—remain few and far between.

The ugliness of modern political campaigns are part of why it can be hard to attract and recruit qualified women for office. While cases like Giselle's are still the exception, not the norm, many women with the qualifications and ambition to run decide not to because they do not want to expose their families to the often-negative realities of a life in politics.

WORK-LIFE BALANCE

The candidate who asked me at the Emerge panel if she could run for office even while having young children was not just asking if it would be practically possible. She was also anxious about her job in the public office taking a backseat to her role as a mom. This is a valid concern and one which should not be overlooked.

Even if a woman is entirely supported by a spouse or able to hire outside resources to cover her domestic responsibilities, many mothers don't want to miss out on nightly family dinners and weekly soccer practices. They want to be there for parent-teacher conferences and piano recitals.

The good news is that politics is becoming more family-friendly. The progress is slow, but it is moving in the right direction. In 2018, the Federal Election Commission approved a petition filed by New York candidate Liuba Grechen Shirley to allow candidates to write off childcare costs as campaign expenses. Hillary Clinton and dozens of members of Congress supported the petition.

Hopefully, women and men will utilize such opportunities. Small changes like this will help level the playing field, eventually breaking the motherhood barrier and allowing women to enter the political arena.

When I asked Florida Senator Lauren Book about her family and what it's like balancing motherhood with a political career, she told me how she often brings her children into her office—coincidentally the same former office of Debbie Wasserman Shultz, who had three young children while serving in the Florida legislature. She also ensures that she hires staffers who support her family-focused lifestyle. Lauren explained that the only way she can "have it all" is through these unorthodox practices.

MOTHERHOOD AS INSPIRATION

While politics is slowly becoming more family-friendly, more women also find that their role as a mother drives them to public service. This was the case for seven-term Washington state assemblywoman Cindy Ryu.

As the owner of a commercial building off Highway 99 in Shoreline, Washington, Cindy was concerned about a measure being considered by the city council to limit access to her building. Though she spoke up at several public hearings, Cindy's concerns fell on deaf ears. Her teenage daughter encouraged her to run for city council to fight the measure.

In 2003, Cindy ran for office and lost to the popular Republican incumbent. However, in 2006, she ran again and won. Then in 2008, she became mayor of Shoreline, the first Korean American woman mayor in the country. In 2010, she ran for and was elected to the state legislature.

During our interview, Cindy shared her original inspiration to run. "When my daughter suggested I run for city council to address the issues facing my business, that sparked something in me. I wanted her to see her mom as someone strong who could make a difference, not just complain about the problems."

Research shows that women are intensely interested in impacting their communities—just like Cindy was. The difference from their male peers is *how* they feel they can make an impact. When asked which path they were most likely to pursue to help improve their community or country, men and women answered equally on their interest in becoming a teacher or getting involved with a religious institution. However, only 15 percent of women chose the option to run for public office, while 28 percent of men chose this option. Forty percent of women chose the opportunity to work for a charity, while only 27 percent of men chose this option.[41]

While working for a charity is a noble path, it's important to note this difference between women's and men's consideration of how they can make an impact. It would benefit women to expand our consideration of all available paths. For example, those interested in volunteer or nonprofit work could consider running for office.

When I speak with female politicians who are also mothers, most of them share the same sentiment as Cindy. Most say that they felt inspired to serve because they wanted to set an example for their daughters or improve the world they passed down to their children. All of these women comment that their experience as a mother makes them better public servants because it gives them a broader perspective on how an issue affects families and children. They have a long-term view of how specific legislation will impact future generations. Viewed in this way, we might come to find that mothers make the best candidates.

REPRESENTATIVE DEMOCRACY

If you have school-aged children (or if you've ever seen a movie that depicts the lives of mothers with school-aged children), you know the everyday makeup of the elementary school Parent-Teachers Association (PTA). It typically consists of hard-working, outspoken women who go above and beyond for their kids. They work tirelessly for their school community to make it safe, meet its educational objectives, and make it an excellent place for all children attending.

Public office is no different. We work tirelessly for the safety and success of our citizens. So why are thousands of PTAs across the country overrun with intelligent, ambitious women, but we don't see these women on local city councils or in state legislatures?

Of course, it's because of the numerous cultural barriers I've been discussing.

While running for PTA president can sometimes be political, doing so does not expose a woman to the media and public scrutiny like running for public office does. A role in the PTA is expected of a woman and is celebrated, whereas a woman running for public office is questioned and ridiculed. The PTA system is designed for passionate parents who want to get involved, whereas the political system is designed for individuals (men) with little to no family responsibilities.

In *Men Rule*, researchers articulate the difference between women's and men's interests at various levels of public office. At a local level, 11 percent of men and 7 percent of women expressed interest in the mayor's office. 26 percent of men expressed interest in serving on the school board compared to 35 percent of women. At the state level, 35 percent of men said they were interested in being a state legislator compared to 25 percent of women. Federal offices had a similar disparity.[42]

So why are women more interested in the school board than other local, state, and federal offices? Experts believe that women feel accepted in those positions where the PTA or the local school board have influence because women already play a vital role in PTAs. There is more of an uphill battle when vying for other offices.

What would happen if these thousands of women suddenly stepped up from the PTA and into their city councils and state assemblies? Not only would men have to do their part to fill in the voids left in the PTA, but we would see a massive wave of competent women applying their energy and influential voices on a higher level. Their impact would benefit not only their children and their schools but their cities, states, and country.

Senior female leaders serving in public office for several decades believe that the environment has improved for women. In *A Seat at the Table*, for example, Senator Dianne Feinstein is quoted as saying, "I see women, younger, able to raise children and do this. I would never have been able to do that."[43] We have more resources available to us now than ever before. The playing field is leveling, and it is gradually becoming more culturally acceptable for a woman to serve in public office, with or without children at home.

Yet, even with these steps forward, significant barriers exist. Regardless of what their home life looks like, women still face more challenges than their male counterparts when it comes to being a public servant and managing a family. Many difficulties can hit quite close to home, and for some women like Giselle Hale, that is a risk they are unwilling to take. But for others, it is a motivator.

Countless women step up to the campaign podium *for* their children and their families because they are passionate about improving their lives and the world around them. Women are called to be a voice for the voiceless, and we hear that call not because we have some grandiose ambition to obtain a particular office or position of power. We step up to serve because we believe in a cause or an issue that affects our families and communities. We want to leave the world better than how we found it for the next generation.

To do so, we often turn discouragement into inspiration. Lauren Book, for example, didn't seek to be the Senate Minority Leader; she enjoyed having autonomy in the process. But there was another male senator who was running for the leadership position with a reputation for being misogynistic. In fact, he said to Lauren, "You can't do the job because you have small children."

This statement made Lauren reconsider her plans. "We are constantly told we can't do it because we're female, we're young, we have children," she said. "If you tell me that I can't do something, I am going to do it."

Lauren decided to run for the leadership position and became the minority leader in 2021. She didn't let the naysayers stop her—instead, she turned their criticism into fuel.

As we know, representative democracy only works if all demographics of the population are represented in government. Therefore we need mothers, non-mothers, fathers, and non-fathers. We need *everyone* to participate in order for all voices to be heard. Make sure you add yours.

CHAPTER 6

MONEY AND POLITICS

"They'll tell you you're too loud, that you need to wait your turn and ask the right people for permission. Do it anyway."
—ALEXANDRIA OCASIO CORTEZ

In November 2022, after a hard-fought campaign and a whopping eight days to tally the votes from the neck-and-neck race, Congresswoman Karen Bass made history as the first female mayor of Los Angeles and the first woman of color to hold the job. It was not the first time she had made history in politics. In 2008, while serving in the California State Assembly, she was the first Black woman elected to serve as speaker of any state legislature.

Karen started her career as a Physician Assistant in the emergency room in Los Angeles, and she credits her mental toughness to that job. She always wanted to be helpful, serve others and prioritize the most vulnerable people in our society. During our interview, she often spoke about her desire to run toward a problem instead of running away from it. This quality is what makes her a unique and successful leader of a major city.

A Los Angeles native, Karen grew up in the Venice and Fairfax neighborhoods of Los Angeles. She was a popular cheerleader at Hamilton High School and always found time to volunteer for community organizing projects. In fact, even before her high school years, Karen explored community service by volunteering for Bobby Kennedy's presidential campaign.

During the 1980s, as an emergency room Physician's Assistant in Los Angeles, Karen saw firsthand the harrowing effects of the crack cocaine epidemic. In response to this crisis, Karen joined forces with local community leaders to establish the Community Coalition, an organization dedicated to tackling drug addiction, crime, and violence in the neighborhoods of South Central Los Angeles.

Karen's mayoral election victory was by no means easy; this 2022 race was one of the most expensive in history. Karen's opponent, Rick Caruso, was an independently successful and charismatic billionaire who spent roughly $107 million on his campaign—eleven times the $9 million raised by Karen. This beat the previous record on personal wealth spent by a mayoral candidate: $102 million by Michael Bloomberg during his 2009 reelection campaign for New York Mayor.

This monetary discrepancy put Karen at a severe disadvantage. I remember sitting with Karen in her hotel suite with her family on election night. We were glued to her laptop, constantly refreshing the Los Angeles registrar of voters website for election result updates. Initial votes put Karen several points behind Rick Caruso.

"Remember," I told her, "The voters will decide who the next Mayor of Los Angeles will be. Not billionaires or corporations."

Karen replied, "I have faith in the voters of Los Angeles."

Our faith was not misplaced. With a strong resume, exceptional leadership traits, and an unwavering platform, Karen ultimately beat her opponent with a campaign budget less than one-tenth the size of his.

Karen's victory demonstrates that raising the most money does not *guarantee* a victory; it is possible to win an election if a candidate raises less than their opponent. However, her victory is an outlier when it comes to the bigger picture of money in politics. While it is possible for the candidate who raises less money to win an election, it is uncommon. Most research on the impact of campaign financing clearly shows a strong correlation between being the better fundraiser and winning the election. According to a study by CAWP reviewing open-seat general election races for single-member districts, the win rate for candidates who outraised their opponents was 74 percent—much higher than the average win rate of 50 percent.[44]

Money is a necessary evil of modern politics. Most candidates—men and women—do not enjoy fundraising, but it is a crucial skill that must be learned and mastered for women to gain true gender parity in government and society, especially if we take the gender wealth gap into account.

The gender wealth gap is a consequence of the fact that women have not been financially independent for long. It's only in the 20th century that women began pursuing financial independence from men. This crucial change granted us numerous personal and professional opportunities: we could open a bank account or credit card without the approval of our father or husband, and we earned the right to control our bodies and make decisions about our health care.

In the 1980s, we took our pursuit of equality to the next level. Women boldly began stepping into positions of power and influence by taking on leadership roles in companies and running for public office. It was no longer the exception for women to work outside the home; in fact, it was even fashionable for women to build careers and obtain high-level positions.

While we no longer have to count on men to take care of us, women have yet to achieve true equality in positions of power. We still have to catch up. We've gained "permission to participate" in government, business, and the economy, but we are nowhere near leading in these realms. For those of us who have lived through the modern evolution of the role of women, it might seem like we've been fighting this fight for a very long time.

The good news is that this work is well underway. But as we continue working toward gender parity, money remains a significant barrier for women in politics.

EARLY MONEY AND DONOR CONFIDENCE

An individual running for a seat in the House or Senate or the office of US President technically becomes a candidate when they raise or spend more than $5,000 on their campaign.[45] However, candidates typically raise at least $1 million for congressional campaigns and up to $7 million for US Senate campaigns. In some states, like California, campaigns for state legislature can cost just as much or even more.

The amount of money a candidate needs to run a successful campaign varies drastically depending on the office, the state, or district, plus several other factors such as the candidate's party affiliation and whether or not they are challenging an incumbent or vying for an open seat, running opposed or unopposed. Regardless, there is one universal truth to all political races: you need money. And ideally, you have a lot of money that you can contribute to your campaign early on.

Candidates who kick off their campaigns with significant money are at a considerable advantage. Having a movement that is well-funded early on leads to additional financial contributions because potential donors see that the candidate has a healthy budget and figure they are more likely to win their race. This increases donor confidence and makes potential donors more inclined to invest their money. After all, large-scale political donations aren't made by individuals who donate just because they like the candidate. This is the motivation behind average citizens who make smaller donations of a few hundred dollars or less, but many high-value donors contribute to candidates to advance their interests once that candidate is in office.

Because of its impact on donor confidence, "early money" is crucial to a candidate's likelihood of winning. As Ellen Malcolm, the founder of EMILY's List, said, "Early Money Is Like Yeast…it makes the dough rise."[46]

This early-money phenomenon is why so many political candidates are independently wealthy. Their chances of winning are much higher because they come to the table already possessing significant funds to back their campaign. It's much easier to run a campaign—and gain additional supporters—if you can pull from your bottomless pockets.

THE WEALTH GAP

Men continue to have much deeper pockets than women. In 2022, just over 13 percent of all billionaires in the United States were female.[47] And of the few women on the list, most of them inherited their wealth or came by it through marriage. Of course, this is a small and very elite selection of individuals, but it represents the unequal distribution of wealth between men and women in our modern society.

As women have entered the workforce and invested more in lucrative careers, we have been striving to make up for lost time that could have been spent accumulating wealth like our male counterparts. But our efforts continue to be hindered. In the twenty-first century, more women are breadwinners than ever before, yet we continue to be paid less than our male counterparts.

The wage gap is a well-known problem in America, as women continue to earn only seventy-nine cents for every dollar men earn. This gap highlights the importance of affordable childcare, universal parental leave, and essential initiatives like equal pay for women. Such advances would immediately level the playing field for women and improve our ability to advance in our careers, build wealth, and, in turn, win political offices.

But the wage gap is a newer issue exacerbating the long-standing, underlying *wealth* gap. Across the general population, women own only thirty-two cents for every dollar owned by our male counterparts.[48] This vast disparity in wealth is a symptom of the many years during which men built wealth and women could not do so. And while we continue to inch our way toward closing this chasm, it has a direct negative impact on women's ability to finance our political campaigns successfully.

According to CAWP's research of open-seat woman versus man contests for state house seats, 46 percent of Democratic men contributed to their campaigns compared to 38 percent of their Republican women opponents. Similarly, 53 percent of Republican men contributed to their campaigns compared to 34 percent of Democratic women opponents.[49] Less able to personally contribute to their campaigns, women have less of the invaluable "early money" which drives subsequent fundraising ability.

THE FUNDRAISING GAP

With less personal wealth to draw from than our male opponents, women face a much steeper uphill battle when it comes to financing their campaigns. We must raise more money, and we have to work harder to do so.

Just as women must prove themselves more than men when applying for a job, female candidates have to prove themselves more than male candidates. The imagination barrier comes into play with donors just as it does with voters: Potential donors see a male candidate and can picture him winning the election. On the other hand, a female candidate must draw a clear picture of her path to victory and go above and beyond to demonstrate that she is a viable candidate. This is the case when she seeks votes from voters and contributions from donors.

For women who enter politics without any prior experience in fundraising, the process can be pretty daunting. For example, in 1990,

Dr. Jean Fuller became the superintendent for the Keppel Union School District in California's Central Valley at forty. Dr. Fuller is a confident, natural leader who worked her way up public education ranks over the following three decades. But as passionate and successful as she was, Dr. Fuller had never run a political campaign until her 2006 bid for State Assembly. When I spoke with Dr. Fuller, she shared the story of feeling quite over her head.

"My mentor, former congressman Bill Thomas, had encouraged me to run for Kevin McCarthy's open seat. Bill gave me campaign fundraising advice, and shortly after, a box arrived on my doorstep at home. I opened it up, and it was full of cards with names and phone numbers and instructions for me to start calling these people and ask them for money!" Dr. Fuller laughs a bit, recalling her feeling of bewilderment.

"I had no script, no guidance, nothing. I'd never worked in sales and had no experience cold-calling people. Talking about myself and asking for money was extremely awkward and unnatural. I remember setting the cards out on my ironing board in my bedroom, and I just looked at them all for a while. But I told myself I could sit here frozen or get good at this cold calling. So I dove in, and I figured it out after a couple of days."

Jean's experience is common for many women running for public office for the first time. During my first campaign, I experienced similar feelings of being lost.

Because of early money's impact on a campaign, the wealth gap between men and women, and the imagination barrier, which skews donor confidence in favor of men, all female candidates start at a disadvantage in races between a man and a woman. There is much more pressure on women to fundraise to successfully compensate for their early disadvantage. And while research shows that women are successful fundraisers who often raise the same *number* of donations as men, the *amount* women receive from donors is typically smaller than what men receive. [50] As a result, women must work harder than their male opponents to raise the same amount of money. That's more phone calls, doors to knock on, and events to attend. It's a numbers game: The more people one can reach, the more money one can raise.

Of course, the larger one's network, the more people one can get. Here, once again, men have an advantage over women.

THE POWER AND INFLUENCE GAP

In a 2015 *New York Times* article titled, "Fewer Women Run Big Companies Than Men Named John," writer Justin Wolfers introduced the Glass Ceiling Index. The index compares the number of chief executives at S&P 1500 firms named John, Robert, William, or James to the number of top female executives at those firms. In 2015, the index was four; for every woman CEO, there were four men named John, Robert, William, or James.[51]

The Times followed up on its Glass Ceiling Index in 2018, with findings that fewer Republican senators were women than men named John, and fewer Democratic governors were women than men named John. It went on to give numerous examples of gender disparity throughout our culture, including the number of female chief executives of Fortune 500 companies being equal to those named James (5 percent). And another staggering statistic: of the most significant tech deals in the previous five years, only 9 percent involved female venture capital investors, compared to 11 percent involving investors named David, James, or Peter.[52]

These findings also unveil something about the gross lack of racial diversity in Corporate America, but we'll come back to that in the next chapter.

As they progress up the corporate ladder, women often opt out of positions of additional responsibility and, along with it, higher rates of pay. This is either by choice, because they don't want to miss out on precious experiences while their children are young, or because they don't have the capacity, like being unable to work a demanding executive job while also managing a busy household. This results in women needing help to pursue a professional opportunity at the same rate as their male peers. It also has the added effect of limiting women's ability to amass wealth and influence at the same level as men. This limitation, as described previously, grossly impacts women's ability to get elected to political office.

RECRUITMENT ORGANIZATIONS FOR WOMEN

Luckily, as more women enter the political arena, we learn more from each other. Organizations like EMILY's List, Women's Political Committee, National Women's Political Caucus, National Organization for Women, and Emerge America continue to pop up to help women in our pursuit of political office.

When EMILY's List was initially founded in 1985, its mission was to drive women's participation in the United States Senate. However, Laphonza Butler, the president of EMILY's List, explained to me that, in recent years, the organization has shifted its focus. Its mission now is to engage women at a more local level to build a pipeline for talent that ultimately reaches the federal level.

"That pipeline starts with local, state legislatures, and constitutional offices," Laphonza said. "That's where we've found the richness of candidates all over the country. We've found numerous women—specifically women of color—working and making great changes in their communities."

When I asked Laphonza what drove her to become more involved in supporting women in politics, her voice became lighter. In the fall of 2020, during the pandemic and just before the November presidential election (a period of political tension in America), Laphonza sat at her kitchen table listening to her six-year-old daughter's kindergarten class hold a mock election.

"The candidates were fun animals like the wolf, the snake, the rooster, and the turtle. We watched the kids cast their ballots by a show of hands, and my kid was the only one out of twenty-three kids in the class who voted for the turtle. I asked her later who won, and she told me the wolf won because he had promised to give the kids candy and more recess time. But I knew she had voted for the turtle, so I asked her why. She said because the turtle had promised to be fair to everyone, that everyone would have an equal chance to play at recess.

"Of course, I was moved by that," Laphonza continued. "I had already been thinking about joining [EMILY's List], and my daughter's reason for voting for the turtle inspired me. I figured I could wake up every day and be a living example of someone helping create the kind of society my daughter longs for."

Laphonza has a personal appreciation for the importance of representation. Growing up in a small town in Mississippi, her family lived paycheck-to-paycheck as her mother worked three different jobs to support Laphonza, her siblings, and their father, who was sick with heart disease.

"I lived the experience of being on government assistance. I witnessed my mom repeatedly making the genuine decision between paying rent or putting food on the table. But I also saw the leadership that was brought forward in my mom. I saw the same thing in the women I worked with at SEIU [Service Employees International Union of California].

I grew up understanding politics through the lens of survival, but I also experienced how survival builds leadership and empathy and brings them to the forefront. Those are the types of people we need leading our communities. And that's who EMILY's List is here to help—help them get elected to office so they can help others."

EMILY's List helps potential candidates through four phases of the election process: by recruiting and developing women who show outstanding leadership potential, by supporting their campaigns with communication and mobilization strategies, by providing relevant research and data about women in politics, and by driving voter participation, especially among women and people of color. EMILY's List is also a PAC that raises money and contributes to campaigns.

Since 1985, the organization has raised over $500 million for political candidates.[53]

Since early money can drive the success of a candidate's campaign, EMILY's List's tactical support, combined with its financial contributions, is a powerful force in helping more women win public offices. In fact, I was fortunate that EMILY's List became more involved in state legislature races in 2006, just when I was running for the California Assembly. EMILY's List reached out to me and offered to provide a staff assistant to support my campaign in the final three months.

However, there is a partisan discrepancy in the support female candidates can access, as many organizations supporting women in politics only support Democratic candidates. For example, EMILY's List only supports pro-choice women. Currently, we have 149 women serving in Congress: 106 are Democrats, 42 are Republicans, and one has no party affiliation. The disparity in the partisan numbers of women representation is largely due to organizations like EMILY's List that proactively recruit and provide resources to women with a specific political affiliation.

Republicans are beginning to set up organizations with a similar infrastructure to EMILY's List. Though Republican donors don't respond to what people call "identity politics," it is encouraging to see younger Republican women leaders starting to engage in more conversations about the value of diversity, recognizing that the country's demographics are changing, and working to proactively support the representation of more women and minorities in Congress.

Congresswoman Elise Stefanik, the youngest woman elected to Congress in 2014, is leading the national effort to increase the number of Republican women elected to Congress. As the first woman to serve as the Recruitment Chair for the National Republican Congressional Committee, she has successfully recruited more than 100 women candidates. Stefanik also helped launch the E-PAC, which was created after the 2018 midterm elections to increase the number of Republican women candidates.

However, recruitment organizations are not the only institutional source of funds for candidates. Political Action Committees (PACs) are one of the most significant alternatives for campaign contributions.

SUPPORT FROM PACS

In the United States, there are roughly five thousand connected PACs, which are formed by an entity such as a corporation or labor union, and approximately two thousand non-connected PACs, created by individuals and independent groups affiliated by common ideology.[54] In the 2018 election, the top ten PACs donated $29,184,565 to federal candidates.[55]

While candidates raise funds from other sources, including individual donors, candidates must gain support from PACs and do so early on in their race. Support from key PACs can solidify a candidate's financial competitiveness and increase their chances of winning. But for women, there are a few unique challenges to gaining support from PACs.

The first challenge is that PACs typically support incumbents. This can be a catch-22 because PACs want to back candidates most likely to win, and incumbents are most likely to win. But perhaps incumbents win more frequently because they have backing from PACs. The same corporations and organizations that lead these PACs are run mostly by powerful men, so the cycle continues: male-led companies donate to PACs, who in turn donate to male candidates and build relationships with the male executives who contributed to their campaigns.

The second challenge women face when gaining support from PACs is the imagination barrier. Like we see at an individual level, collective organizations like PACs have trouble envisioning a woman in elected office, even in open-seat contests where there is no incumbent. All other variables being equal, backing a female candidate is a greater risk for PACs than supporting a male candidate.

Lastly, PACs are more likely to back a candidate who brings their financial contributions to the table and has a significant personal network and influence. But as we've seen, men tend to have more personal wealth and connections than women, so in this regard also, male candidates tend to win the favor of PACs.

Fortunately, dozens of PACs have been created with the strategic mission of supporting female and minority candidates, and more are entering the fray every election cycle.

WHAT HOLDS US BACK

The imagination barrier doesn't only impact donors. In fact, when it comes to fundraising, the imagination barrier also impacts the female candidates themselves. Research shows that women are more averse to fundraising than men. According to the CAWP study *Poised to Run*, "most women believe that it is harder for female candidates to raise money than male candidates, while the overwhelming majority of men believe it is equally hard for both men and women."[56]

Our perceived disadvantage may be due to our "good girl" mentality. For women raised to be "good girls," asking for money feels entirely improper.

My relationship with money is a complicated one. I was brought up to never discuss money and never ask for any; under no circumstances would I ever bring that kind of shame upon my family. So when I accepted my first professional job at the Asian Law Caucus, I didn't even ask about compensation during the interview process. When the human resources manager began telling me about the pay and benefits package, I listened uncomfortably.

At a later job with MetLife Insurance, I informed my manager that I was leaving for a new position at a different company. She was shocked because I had never expressed any concern about my position. She asked if it was a matter of money, and I reluctantly told her that money was partly the issue and that the new job was offering me more. My manager told me she would have given me more money if I had said something, but it had never even crossed my mind to ask. I had been taught to be grateful for my opportunities and to not come across as greedy by asking about money.

As a candidate, I had to build a bridge from my cultural upbringing of never discussing money to making cold calls. I had some experience fundraising for my nonprofit work, for which I had raised over $10 million, but raising money for oneself is very different from raising money for a cause. Still, I learned to do it anyway.

DO IT ANYWAY

In their guidebook titled *Keys to Elected Office*, the Barbara Lee Family Foundation summarizes the systemic financial barriers facing female candidates as follows:[57]

The Challenge

Although women now often regularly raise and spend money in their campaigns on par with their male opponents, women candidates still report being excluded from financial circles that include the wealthiest and best-connected donors.

These circles are often based around corporate associations and specific industries—talk about old boys' clubs—and rarely include many women executives or board members. As a result, there are fewer women to make introductions and open doors.

Women may also find they need to wage a "campaign of belief" with donors and spend time highlighting their path to victory.

The Solution

Well before a decision to run, women should be meeting with key allies and honing their campaign skills. This will enable them to hit the ground running, which we know is critical for women's success with voters.

Women's campaign teams should be sure to over-budget the time spent fundraising, and the candidate should be prepared to convince donors that she is worth the investment.

When I interviewed Laphonza Butler, president of EMILY's List, I asked her what women can do to overcome these systemic barriers. Her response was quick and confident. She simply said, "Do it anyway."

"Women tend to look at our opportunities from a place of lack," Laphonza went on to explain. "We think either we don't have the financial resources, or we lack a certain set of skills or experience. But we need to focus on what we *do bring* to the table. You have the lived experience of advocating for your aging parent in a nursing home or of working for your local school. Your journey prepares you. So, even if you lack certain knowledge or resources, do it anyway. For the rest of it, that's what organizations like EMILY's List are for."

If you're inclined to run, do not feel limited by what you lack. Instead, reach out for support and utilize the many resources available to you. Focus on what you *do* bring to the table. Even if you are at a disadvantage compared to wealthy and well-connected male opponents, *do it anyway.*

CHAPTER 7

RACIAL BIAS

**"I am not free while any woman is unfree,
even when her shackles are very different from my own."**

—AUDRE LORDE

W hen my family and I moved from South Korea to Southern California, there were not many Asian families living in our new community. Most of the kids at my school were blonde with blue eyes and had solid Californian accents. It's hard enough trying to fit into the crowd in seventh grade, but it's extra challenging when you arrive from the other side of the world, looking completely different and speaking a foreign language. The kids (and many adults) in Orange County had never seen anyone like me.

That is, except for on the evening news.

Connie Chung was my idol, so I didn't mind much when the kids called me "Connie" in a teasing manner. She wasn't the worst thing they could have compared me to. But I know now, as an adult, that when these kids faced me, they were facing an imagination barrier. They did not see many Asian people, let alone interact with or develop meaningful relationships with them. In reality, the only Asian person my classmates "knew" was Connie Chung, and she was just some news lady on TV—a talking head. For those kids, it was difficult to believe there was a place for an Asian girl at Hewes Junior High School.

While some kids grappled with their imagination barrier in silence, others felt a need to express their internal disconnect outwardly, like calling me "Connie." At the root of their behavior was a lack of understanding and a fear of something with which they were unfamiliar. The kids in my Orange County community did not understand Asians; we arrived from a faraway country that they knew very little about, so they chose to diminish me to make themselves feel safer.

Similarly, while our democratic process gives all citizens in all communities the right to vote and the right to run for office, there are numerous cultural, systemic, and real racial barriers keeping people of color from reaching public office. The very people who should be representing these communities cannot do so, and their needs continue to go unmet. These racial barriers compound the many other obstacles faced by all women, making it even harder for minority women to achieve positions of power and leadership. This is the case with our ability to receive endorsements, raise campaign money, and win votes.

As described by the CAWP study, *The Money Race for the State Legislature*, "Women of color have lagged white women historically in politics including state legislative officeholding. In part, the constraints facing women of color candidates matter early in the process because of limited, favorable electoral opportunities. And a growing body of evidence suggests that the intersection of gender and race puts women of color at a greater disadvantage in the money race. If women candidates from historically underrepresented racial/ethnic groups lack donor confidence about their viability, personal financial resources, and access to moneyed networks, they may be disadvantaged relative to white women."[58]

A study conducted by OpenSecrets, a nonpartisan, nonprofit research group dedicated to following the money in politics, reported that despite a record number of women running, contributing, and voting during the 2020 congressional election cycle, racial and gender inequalities in fundraising remain a barrier of entry for many women of color candidates, particularly in primary elections. For example, Black Democratic women received much less money than other candidates from early donors. According to coauthors Grace Haley and Sarah Bryner, "White men running for office consistently dominate in fundraising. Whatever fundraising advantages may help women seem to primarily help white women, and whatever fundraising advantages may help people of color seem to primarily help men."[59]

Women candidates often rely on women donors for early support, but women on average donate half as much to Black women, Latina women, Indigenous women, MENA women, and Asian and Pacific Islander women candidates as they give to white women. Black women raised on average a third of what white women raised in competitive primaries, and white women had the highest totals in their average total receipts, average amount from PACs, average individual donations.[60] Women of color candidates are consistently left behind.

In my conversation with Laphonza Butler, president of EMILY's List, she described the result of the racial barriers in national politics. "Right now, no Black women are serving in the US Senate. Even while conversations of civil rights, voting rights, and debates about childcare are happening in the chamber, there is no one representing the lives and experiences of Black women. And that's true for many other groups."

Laphonza went on to observe, "Sometimes we get to a place as a society where we feel like if there is one person of a certain demographic, we think we've accomplished something. We think if there's one Latina, then the entirety of the Latino community is represented.

And that one person must carry the burden of representing all of those people in this country. If we want to build a truly representative democracy then we have a lot more work to do, particularly in the space of women of color."

MISIDENTIFICATION

When Fiona Ma and I joined the California State Assembly in 2006, we were among a few Asian American women. During the next six years, people often mixed us up, calling me "Fiona" and Fiona "Mary." Of course, these accidental mix-ups were unintentional, and to make things less awkward for everyone, Fiona and I usually just laughed them off.

On one occasion, I was called to present my bill to the State Senate Local Government Committee. As I sat down at the witness table and began to speak, the committee chair, a white female Senator, interrupted and asked me where Mary Hayashi was. I had to politely let her know that I was Mary Hayashi.

On another occasion, one of the few Asian women lobbyists in Sacramento was eating breakfast alone at a local cafe when a health-care lobbyist approached her. Once he began speaking to her about how he would be testifying at the Business and Professions Committee that morning, she quickly realized he thought that she was me.

Fiona and I are not alone in being mistaken for someone of the same race. In fact, author Angela Yang, writing for NBC News, asserts that misidentification is common for Asian Americans in public life.[61]

For example, Boston Mayor Michelle Wu, a Taiwanese American, is often confused with Beth Huang, the Korean American Massachusetts Voter Table Executive Director. Once, NBC News reported that a protester wanting to get his message out to Mayor Michelle Wu began yelling at Beth instead. And this isn't the first time this had happened to Beth—nor was it the first time another Asian American woman had been confused with Michelle Wu.[62]

And it isn't only individuals who misidentify other people. ABC World News Tonight misidentified New York City community organizer Grace Lee as Michelle Go, an Asian American woman who was pushed in front of a subway train in January of 2022. Later, ABC World News stated that the misidentification was a technical error, not due to insensitivity.

A study done by Brent Hughes at U.C. Riverside suggests that people identify faces from their own race better. But our bias against other races begins as soon as we see someone from another race but don't proceed to the next level (i.e., distinguish them from that group as the unique and separate individual that they are).[63]

"Every time that happens, it's not intentional," stated Beth Huang, in her interview with NBC News. "Or I assume it's not intentional. But it does make me think that, often, we are not perceived to be as valuable as individual leaders."[64]

As harmless as these types of slip-ups seem, they outwardly demonstrate what's going on in the mind of the individual who makes them. The person who inadvertently conflated Fiona and me, for example, was so unaccustomed to engaging with Asian women that they subconsciously perceived us as identical. This is not the same as the old stereotypical assumption that "all Asians look alike to white people." The underlying problem is that the person knows so few Asian women—and at such a superficial level—that the few Asian women they do know hold no place of distinct recognition in their mind.

In other words, misidentification contributes to an individual's sense of invisibility, of not being seen as they are, for who they are and for the talents they bring to the table. In public office, where leadership is vital and the perception of leadership can make or break your chances of being elected, such misidentification undermines a person's confidence.

The same is true for the workplace. A study published in Jama Network showed that Black, Hispanic, and Native American resident physicians in the US are "routinely mistaken for other minority residents," which contributes to increased workplace stress.[65] Being confused with another person of the same race by someone at a workplace can happen to anyone, but experts say misidentification happens more often to people of color in majority-white spaces.[66]

"Equality Matters," a series by BBC News, reported that in 2019, an Australian magazine ran a story on South Sudan-born model Adut Akech Bior but printed a photo of another black model, Flavia Lazarus. At the Oscars in 2021, a South African reporter asked *Judas and the Black Messiah* star Daniel Kaluuya, who won Best Supporting Actor, how he felt about being "directed by Regina," but Regina King had directed fellow nominee Leslie Odom Jr. in *One Night in Miami*. Sir Lenny Henry, America Ferrera, and Samuel L. Jackson have also been mistaken for other celebrities of the same racial groups.[67]

Have you ever started a new job or joined a new social circle where two or more of the people in the group look similar, have similar mannerisms, or for some reason remind you of each other? In the beginning, it might have been hard to remember who was who, but as time went on, you learned more about each person so that they became distinctive in your mind. Well, this is what was *not* happening for those who inadvertently mixed up Fiona and me. They had yet to give one or both of us enough of their mental bandwidth to solidify us as distinctly different people in their minds.

Occasionally, the inability to distinguish between individuals arises from limited exposure or unfamiliarity. However, there were times when, even after working with both Fiona and me for extended periods, some colleagues *still* couldn't differentiate between us. Continuous mix-ups, especially when colleagues seem uninterested in learning our names, can be emotionally draining. This behavior hints at a deeper, systemic issue: a belief that the distinction simply isn't significant enough to note.

STEREOTYPING

When I joined the California state legislature, I was once again the foreign "new kid" who challenged the imagination barriers of others.

By that time, my Korean accent was gone; I had even glossed over it with a touch of Southern California "valley girl" inflection during my teenage years in Orange County. I was far more American than I was Korean. Plus, I had been working for nonprofits and other political interests for years. I was just as accomplished and qualified as the rest of the people in the state legislature, but I *looked* different.

Most of the people I interacted with had little prior experience with Asian women—at work or in their personal lives. For many of them, their experience with Asian women was in stereotypical roles: their server at a restaurant, the checkout person at the grocery store, or the caregiver in a nursing home. Hardly any of the men I regularly encountered in the State Assembly were used to engaging with an Asian woman as an intellectual peer. They were unfamiliar with my background and my beliefs. Some of them probably even wondered how well I spoke English. This made them very uneasy when attempting to discuss policy issues with me. My mere presence challenged their imagination barrier.

My colleagues were not unusual in their limited views on Asian Americans. In 2021, LAAUNCH, an organization that engages Asian Americans to fight racism and discrimination, commissioned a national study about the attitudes and perceptions of Asian Americans. After polling 2,766 American adults across the country, they found that 42 percent of Americans could not name a well-known Asian American. Among those who did name someone, the most popular choices were martial arts figures such as Jackie Chan (11 percent) and Bruce Lee (9 percent), who died more than fifty years ago.[68]

To further complicate things, I was also forcing myself to step out of my "good girl" role. I was pushing myself to demonstrate bold mannerisms and to speak my mind with clarity and confidence. These traits flew in the face of every stereotype my colleagues possessed about Asian women, making it even harder for them to break down their imagination barriers and figure out how to interact with me.

The braver, more confident men and women were able to overcome their imagination barrier. After a few interactions, they realized I was an educated American who had been elected to serve U.S. citizens. They saw me for *who* I am rather than *what* country I came from, and they treated me as a competent professional. But a few men (and women) remained beholden to their unconscious bias. They were unable to engage with me properly, an Asian woman.

Apart from the mental toll these sorts of interactions exact on a person of color, it makes it hard for that person to do their job effectively. We all exist in a network of human relationships, and it's difficult to function within your nexus if those around you cannot fully accept the role you are in or recognize the value you bring to the table. Worse, much of this stereotyping is subtle, existing as an undercurrent to everyday conversations or interactions, leaving the person emotionally and mentally depleted—and with the task of articulating the stereotyping so that it can be addressed.

COVERT RACISM AND THE "MODEL MINORITY"

In the spring of 2010, I attended a legislative reception for an influential business association in Sacramento. The organization was one of the top supporters of the consumer protection legislation I had authored. During the reception, after I was introduced, the executive of the association smiled, shook my hand, and said, "I didn't realize the author of our bill was a cute oriental!"

Fortunately, this type of overtly ignorant behavior has become increasingly taboo throughout our society. Most people—especially professionals—know not to make such comments. But I've found that while it is widely known that such overt racism toward Black and Latino people is unacceptable, the same sensitivity is not readily offered toward Asian people. In fact, according to a LAAUNCH study, almost 80 percent of Asian Americans say they do not feel respected and are discriminated against in the United States.[69] The latest STAATUS Index Report indicates that one in two Asian Americans feels unsafe in their communities because of race/ethnicity; furthermore, Asian American women are among the least likely of all racial groups to feel belonging and acceptance in America. Among many contributing factors for not feeling a sense of belonging include racial discrimination experiences and not seeing others like themselves in positions of power. [70]

Asian Americans are often referred to as the "model minority." Along with a few relatively harmless negative stereotypes, such as being bad drivers, we are labeled with positive stereotypes like being innovative and hard-working. Because these stereotypes have positive connotations, it's assumed that we don't require the same level of consideration as other minorities.

Of course, it's not a competition to see which minority gets treated with more or less sensitivity. But the lack of consideration given to Asians genuinely impacts those who are public figures, including elected officials.

While the Asian stereotype of being "good at math" isn't harmful, it can limit our opportunities. For example, John Chiang served as Treasurer of California from 2015 to 2019. With an early career as a tax law specialist for the IRS, John had a relatively easy time proving his academic credentials. People saw an Asian man in a mathematical field, and they didn't have any doubts. But when John first started running for elected offices, he repeatedly had to prove his leadership qualities since traditional traits like strength and assertiveness are not typically associated with Asians.

Such a reaction to minority candidates is not overtly racist. It's not as apparent as the executive who smiled and called me a "cute oriental" to my face. But because of this, it is harder to identify and confront. Rather than spouting them to your face, those who possess racist thoughts and biases harbor them quietly within themselves.

Unfortunately, the COVID-19 pandemic brought to the surface much of the long-sleeping hatred for Asians. President Trump's constant referral to COVID-19 as the China Virus," for example, sparked a wave of despicable bullying, harassment, and hate crimes across the country, highlighting how our society uses race as a scapegoat for anything unpleasant. The Anti-Defamation League reported an 84 percent increase in negative statements on Twitter towards Asians following these comments by President Trump.

The 2022 documentary, *The Race Epidemic*, by executive producer John Kobara, highlights the challenges faced by Asian American representatives and lawmakers. For example, during campaigns for public office, there are no repercussions when extremely negative campaigning is used against Asian American candidates, while there would be if the same approach were taken against Black or Latino candidates. Since Asians are the "model minority," it's acceptable to demonstrate hatred and injustice towards them.

As stated in the documentary, *Who's the Asian Jesse Jackson? Who's the Asian Al Sharpton?* Asians don't have the exact representation and, in turn, don't garner the same sensitivity as other minority races.

THE ISSUE OF COMPOUNDING

As disrespectful as this demonstration of the imagination barrier can be to someone on a personal level, the biggest issue is the effect it has on voters. Just as the general population has a hard time imagining women in public office, it has an even harder time envisioning a *woman of color* in public office.

For women of color, compounding worsens all of the barriers women face when attempting to enter public office. For example, women are considered weaker leaders than men, and Asian women are considered passive and meek—two traits not typically associated with a strong leader. So, if an Asian woman stands on the podium next to a white male, the compounding effect of the electorate's imagination barriers is extreme. They have a tough time seeing the Asian woman as a strong leader, even next to a white woman, and especially next to a white man.

What happens when I speak out about disagreements on public policy issues? During my tenure in the California State Assembly, people sometimes described me as "aggressive" or "very competitive." On the other hand, male legislators with solid opinions were applauded as "strong committee chairs" and "brilliant policy experts."

Ruchika Tulshyan, an expert on diversity and women's leadership in the workplace, said, "We're often expected to be submissive and grateful, often navigating much narrower expectations of what it means to be a 'likable' professional woman. And often, Asian women are penalized when they present as a counter to this stereotype."

The same thing is happening in corporate America. An article by *USA Today* observes, "Asian women are often seen as too deferential and submissive to run business lines or companies," just as they're seen in public office. "Asian women are half as likely as white women to be executives, on par with Black and Hispanic women." No S&P 100 companies have an Asian woman as their CEO, and only four of the Fortune 500 companies' CEOs are Asian women.[71]

According to the US Census Bureau, Asian Americans are the best-educated and highest-earning racial or ethnic group in the United States. However, *USA Today* also found that while Asian workers are more likely than any other major racial group to hold a managerial job in the S&P 100, the rates are much lower for Asian women than for Asian men. Ellen Pao, co-founder and CEO of Project Include, whose mission is to increase diversity in the technology sector, believes that the lack of representation of Asian women in leadership positions is viewed as a personal failing rather than a systemic barrier.

One of these systemic barriers is the gender pay gap. The gender pay gap affects women of all races and ethnicities, but women of color face an even more significant pay disparity than their white female counterparts, making it a critical issue of intersectional inequality. For example, Latinas, on average, are paid 46 percent less than white men and 26 percent less than white women.[72] Even though Latinas are attending college at higher rates than ever before, it hasn't eliminated the pay gap; Latinas with a bachelor's degree earn 31 percent less than white men on average.[73]

Because of the stereotype that Latinas are domestic workers in lower-paying jobs—and not ambitious in their careers—many employers think that they don't expect to be paid well.[74] But even when they're holding the same job, Latinas are paid less than their white male counterparts. For example, Latina nurses earn 25 percent less than white men nurses while often experiencing sexism and racism in the workplace—specifically the stereotype that they are less competent than men and less smart than white people.[75] This perception is, of course, false. In fact, Latinas are overrepresented in front line jobs, including providing critical services during the COVID-19 pandemic.[76] Unfortunately, the wage gap results in an average lifetime loss of $1,163,920 for a Latina worker.[77]

In my interview with Connie Perez-Andreesen, a Certified Public Accountant and former congressional candidate for CD 21, Connie recalled a conversation with a work colleague during a work trip. He said, "You won't make partner. Look at the makeup of the firm—they are all white and mostly male." He then suggested she should get a job with the county, where she could earn good benefits.

That wasn't the first time Connie suffered from such discrimination and gatekeeping. Connie's parents, Jesus and Consuelo Perez, came to the United States from Mexico in 1975 to work in the fields of Central Valley in California. Her mother was pregnant with her at the time, and the family settled in the Woodville Farm Labor Camp, about eight miles west of Porterville. Just before graduating from college, Connie applied to several accounting firms—but not the most prominent and influential regional accounting firm. Why?

Connie explained, "This is the most influential accounting firm in the region. They wouldn't hire someone like me, a Mexican from a farm labor camp." But one of her professors encouraged her to apply anyway. Not only did the prestigious firm hire her, Connie went on to manage the accounts of major governmental, agricultural, and petroleum companies.

She also became one of only two Latinas to make partner in its forty-year history.

Connie's experience underscores the profound impact that deep-rooted stereotypes and biases can have on individual perceptions and opportunities. And such prejudices are not confined to any single ethnic or racial group. To further illustrate this, consider the challenges faced by Black women.

The erroneous stereotype that paints Black women as frequently hostile, aggressive, illogical, and bitter, creates a misconception that can impede Black women's genuine contributions and potential in professional settings. Research from the *Harvard Business Review* reveals a distinct bias in how individuals are treated when expressing anger at work.[78] While there's scant evidence indicating Black women are inherently angrier than their white counterparts, they face heightened scrutiny when they display anger, reinforcing the misguided "angry Black woman" trope. This racial bias manifests in various ways, from less favorable job evaluations to limited leadership opportunities . Moreover, the economic disparity is striking: Black women earn just sixty-three cents for every dollar that non-Hispanic white men make. Over the course of a forty-year career, that's an average loss of over $960,000 for Black women workers.[79]

For Native American women, accurate and timely government data sources about gender pay gaps are not always readily available. But what we do know from a National Women's Law Center's fact sheet is that Native American women are paid sixty cents for every dollar paid to white, non-Hispanic men.[80] This wage gap will result in a nearly $1 million loss for Native American women during their lifetime.

It is essential to recognize and address the gender pay gap for women of color to promote workplace fairness, equity and justice. Gender and racial biases, and the resulting stereotypes, have real consequences for the lives of countless women and their families.

LACK OF INSTITUTIONAL SUPPORT

Compounding similarly impacts the support women of color receive (or, I should say, don't receive) from party leaders and others in their circle of influence. As we discussed, the CAWP found that about one-third of women legislators say someone tried to discourage them from running—most often an officeholder or political party official. But of particular concern is that women of color were even more likely than their non-Hispanic white female Democratic colleagues in the state houses to have encountered an effort to discourage them from running—42 percent versus 28 percent.[81] Racial barriers and gender stereotypes can be major negative factors when women of color run for public office.[82]

Both data points are disappointing. No woman should be discouraged from running for office.

Suppose all other factors, like party affiliation, are equal. In that case, the only reason women of color are discouraged from running more often than white women has to be because of their race. Party leaders are either preventing them unconsciously—letting their imagination barriers get the best of them—or they're doing it consciously because they believe a woman of color cannot win. Often, party leaders make assumptions about voter attitudes and perceptions about women candidates, and those assumptions about viability can create challenges for women of color.

Leah Wright Rigueur, a professor of US History at Brandeis University, said, " When [women] do run, they are often overwhelmingly outspent by white men who have access to 'networks' and 'war chests' of wealth and power. One of the things that we know is that women of color are often discouraged from running for politics because they don't have war chests that rival their male counterparts." Leah also noted that sexism and racism have historically marginalized women and women of color from fully participating in the political system.

In her interviews with the first Democratic women of color congressional candidates, Deena Zaru of Good Morning America observed that these three women shattered this perception of a successful political candidate: (1) Rep. Veronica Escobar, one of the first Latinas to represent Texas in Congress; (2) Rep. Ilhan Omar, one of only two Muslim women in Congress; and (3) Rep. Deb Haaland, one of the first Native American women in Congress.[83] In 2018, these women made history as they were sworn into the 116th class of lawmakers.

During her primary election, Debra Haaland faced five other candidates, including another woman, so she did not receive any support from organizations like EMILY's List. This made fundraising difficult from the start. Similarly, when Rep. Omar decided to run for Congress in 2018, she ran against five opponents, including two women. She clearly did not have the fundraising advantage as compared to other candidates in the race. However, she prevailed in Minnesota's 5th district, a majority-white Democratic stronghold, by fundraising small, individual donations for her campaign.

At age twenty-nine, Alexandria Ocasio-Cortez drew national attention when she became the youngest woman ever to serve in the United States Congress. While working as a bartender and first time candidate for Congress, she defeated Democratic Caucus Chair Joe Crowley, a ten-year incumbent. It was considered the biggest upset victory in the 2018 midterm election primaries.

Ocasio-Cortez did not accept corporate contributions but rather relied on grassroots donors to finance her campaign. Her opponent had all the fundraising advantages as an incumbent and had secured high-profile endorsements from Governor Cuomo and the two US Senators from New York, Chuck Schumer and Kirsten Gillibrand. Despite being outspent by a margin of eighteen to one ($1.5 million to $83,000), Alexandria Ocasio-Cortez won with 57.13 percent of the vote compared to her opponent's 42.5 percent.

UNDERREPRESENTATION

As a result of compounding barriers, the problem of underrepresentation is much worse for women of color than it is for women as a whole. Black women make up 6.8 percent of Americans but only 4.61 percent of state legislators. Latinas make up 9.6 percent of Americans but only 1.81 percent of state legislators. Asian and Pacific Islander women comprise 3.3 percent of Americans but less than 1 percent of state legislators.[84]

Underrepresentation is just as poor at the federal level. Only three out of one hundred US Senators are women of color.[85] As of this book's publication, there are no Black women currently serving in the US Senate. In fact, to date, only two Black women have ever been elected to the US Senate.[86] While a record number of Latinas and Black women joined the House of Representatives in 2023, no Middle Eastern, North African, or Native woman has yet been elected to serve in the US Senate.[87] It's worse still in executive offices, where only twelve out of fifty governors are women, and only one is a woman of color.[88]

But the issue of underrepresentation is more than just a matter of statistics—the actual impact on underserved communities is dire. The CDC study I discovered in the 1990s that overlooked the use of tobacco among Asian Americans would have driven flawed decision-making about the allocation of government resources to help people at risk from tobacco use. Had I not decided to challenge the CDC's findings, Asian Americans would have gone without the support and resources they badly needed. Similarly, without proper representation, underserved communities requiring the most help are less likely to receive it if no one representing them understands their needs or is looking out for their interests.

It is crucial for party leaders and civic institutions to proactively recruit qualified women who show excellent leadership potential. We then must support them in their campaigns for public office by helping them break down the countless barriers they face that many of their opponents do not. By providing additional help to those who are currently underrepresented, we improve the democratic process for everyone.

As we continue to recruit qualified women to run for public office, the ballot will reflect a complete representation of our society. As there are more diverse candidates to choose from, the number of voters legitimately choosing women will increase. As a result, more of us will take office, and we will achieve more diverse representation.

CHAPTER 8

THE ROLE OF THE MEDIA

"[When a woman is elected into office] it breaks down
the [imagination] barrier in voters' minds and helps voters
reimagine what leadership roles look like, and opens the door
for women at all levels in politics."

—AMANDA HUNTER

During the 2008 US Presidential election, Tina Fey, a senior cast member on NBC's *Saturday Night Live*, created an uncanny portrayal of Republican vice presidential candidate Sarah Palin. Along with her friend and fellow *SNL* cast member Amy Poehler—who had established an excellent Hillary Clinton impression years earlier—Tina Fey appeared in a sketch about the political rivals at a mock press conference.

The characters stated they were crossing party lines and holding the joint press conference to address "the repulsive role that sexism is playing in the campaign." The Hillary Clinton character states,

"I believe that diplomacy should be the cornerstone of any foreign policy," to which the Sarah Palin character responds, "and I can see Russia from my house!" in an overly-perky voice.

Sarah Palin never actually said, "I can see Russia from my house." What she stated was, "You can actually see Russia from land here in Alaska, from an island in Alaska." It was an entirely true statement. But the real quote, and its accuracy, didn't align with the bimbo angle the media had created for her.

The joke immediately became a pop culture phenomenon and cemented Sarah Palin's caricature as an uninformed beauty queen.

SNL is known to be a liberal media machine, so no one would expect the show's producers to overtly support a conservative figure like Sarah Palin, but cultural pillars like *SNL* undoubtedly affect how women are perceived and treated in our society. They could have the power to help tear down the imagination barrier by portraying women as competent, but in this case, they let Tina Fey's funny yet exaggerated depiction of Sarah Palin translate into an actual negative perception of the female leader.

In an article titled "The 'Bitch' and the 'Ditz,'" published by *New York Magazine* in November 2008, author Amanda Fortini reflected on how the media and, in fact, the country, treated these two very different female political leaders throughout the unprecedented election.[89]

Amanda wrote, "[Hillary Clinton] was highly competent, serious, diligent, prepared (sometimes overly so)—a woman who cloaked her femininity in hawkishness and pantsuits. But she had, to use an unfortunate term, likability issues, and she inspired in her detractors an upwelling of sexist animus: She was likened to Tracy Flick for her irritating entitlement and Lady Macbeth for her boundless ambition. You get the idea she was a grind, scold, harpy, shrew, press, teacher's pet, and a killjoy. She was repeatedly called a bitch (as in: 'How do we beat the…') and a buster of balls."

In contrast, Sarah Palin was a relatively unknown female leader who came onto the scene unexpectedly as John McCain's running mate. But while there was initial excitement for this seemingly competent woman, that excitement quickly turned into disappointment when, after several interview blunders, Sarah demonstrated that she might not be qualified to be second-in-command.

"By stepping into the spotlight unprepared," Amanda wrote, "Palin reinforced some of the most damaging and sexist ideas of all: that women are undisciplined in their thinking; that we are distracted by domestic concerns or frivolous pursuits like shopping; that we are not smart enough, or not serious enough, for the important jobs."

While Sarah Palin may not have been qualified for the job, her portrayal in the media was undoubtedly much worse than she deserved, and the harsh portrayal furthered the stereotype of women in leadership.

Amanda Fortini went on to observe that, while Hillary Clinton and Sarah Palin are just two individual women, their treatment during the 2008 election had great importance. "...because so few women are present at the highest levels of government, they carry the burden of representing their gender more so than men. In politics and business, an unqualified woman does more damage than no woman. She serves to fortify the stereotypes that the next woman will have to surmount."

The media's portrayal of Hillary and Sarah during the 2008 presidential election reinforced the perception that women's role in society is binary: that we can be either "the bitch" or "the ditz" or, as Amanda Fortini put it, "the hard-ass or the lightweight, the battle-ax or the bubblehead, the serious, pursed-lipped shrew or the silly, ineffectual girl."

It remains difficult for women—especially those in the public eye—to be perceived as well-educated yet down-to-earth, strong but humanly kind. Instead, we're cast as either entirely masculine or consumingly feminine, overqualified or inexperienced. There's no option in between. Such binarism makes it impossible for women to achieve gender parity.

If we continue to accept these offensive portrayals of female leaders, we will never break down society's imagination barrier of the role of women. If we keep making excuses for the mocking, ridicule, and sexualization of women in our media and entertainment, then nothing will change. Young girls will continue to see this treatment of women who step into the spotlight and decide against ever doing the same. The stereotype that women are too weak or incompetent to serve in leadership roles will remain firmly in place, and so will the imagination barrier.

A WOMAN'S APPEARANCE

The media's portrayal of women directly impacts our ability to campaign and win public office. During the height of her political career, Hillary Clinton's hair was the subject of endless commentary, and she was constantly criticized for having a cold attitude. California gubernatorial candidate Meg Whitman was constantly asked about plastic surgery. In 2005, Secretary of State Condoleezza Rice was called a "dominatrix" for visiting an Army airfield in a sleek black trench coat and knee-high leather boots.

In her documentary, *Miss Representation*, Jennifer Newsom says, "[If] the media are so derogatory to the most powerful women in the country, then what does it say about our ability to take any woman in America seriously?" She also explored the media's impact on young girls, who constantly see a woman's value determined by her sex appeal rather than her academic or professional contributions.[90]

Today's young women believe that, yes, they can do things like be a CEO or run for President, but they also must look good doing it. Otherwise, they will be criticized. At best, they will feel valued because, in addition to being intelligent and competent, they also happen to be pretty. At worst, their accomplishments will be overshadowed by any slight peculiarity in their appearance.

Unfortunately, even when a woman does everything right in her campaign, the media can still tear her down and unravel all her excellent work. Even when she develops and holds to an authentic "brand," as Amanda Hunter of the Barbara Lee Foundation recommended, research shows that when the media mentions a woman's appearance in any way—whether the commentary is positive or negative—voters' perception of her as a leader plummets. The mere mention of her appearance draws voters' attention to the fact that she is a woman, reminding them of their unconscious bias, which says women cannot be leaders. The same issue does not exist for men.

MISINFORMATION

"The rumor about Mayor Wu having panic attacks is false," Amanda Hunter said. "Questioning Mayor Wu's mental health is a direct attack on her strength as a leader."

Michelle Wu, thirty-six, is Boston's first Asian American mayor. Her victory marks significant progress for the Asian American community. "Growing up, I never thought I would or should be involved in politics," Mayor Wu said while speaking to reporters at the election night event in Boston. "I didn't see anyone who looked like me in spaces of power. We are redefining what leadership looks like."

Since becoming the Mayor of Boston, Michelle Wu has experienced several insidious attacks on her character, including a false rumor questioning her stability and mental health. One story claimed that Mayor Wu, overwhelmed by the pressures of her job and the protestors outside of her home, suffered several panic attacks and was taken by ambulance to a hospital. Of course, there's no record of any emergency calls or an ambulance being dispatched to her home. The mayor responded by saying that she has never been hospitalized for a panic attack but would not hesitate to seek help if she were in distress.

Unfortunately, this false claim was not only spread online via social media, but on January 15, a newspaper published a feature story on Mayor Wu experiencing a panic attack years earlier as she was battling anxiety about becoming a public figure. Though *The*

Boston Globe investigated the claim and found it entirely false, it shows that critics are willing to use the stigma of mental illness to attack the leadership of a woman and a person of color. Experts say this type of misinformation is often used to make qualified candidates and officials seem unfit for public office.

STYLE OVER SUBSTANCE

One of the most damaging ways in which the media affects women is the language they use to report on female leaders' actions or noteworthy events. Male candidates and legislative leaders do not need to worry about if they are "feminine enough" or "too masculine." But women in politics consistently face these judgements. Indeed, no matter what they do, their behavior, tone, speech, and even their political priorities are analyzed and interpreted through a "feminine" lens, with the media using terms and language that emphasize women's traditional roles.

When Karen Bass served as Speaker of the Assembly, a story in the *Los Angeles Times* surfaced with the headline, "A Target atop the Assembly." It claimed, "The Assembly's den mother became a growling bear, griping after an unsuccessful budget session between legislative leaders and the governor." The article went on to report that her vocal critics complained about Karen's "wishy-washy administrative style" and that she was "politically tone deaf."[91]

The language used was associated with traditional gender roles and outdated concepts of the "feminine," making it difficult for Karen to convey to the public that she was a serious and qualified assembly leader (an issue faced by many other women leaders before her). These derogatory race and gender portrayals and treatment continued to be pervasive in her career. Karen was often characterized as a "therapist," interested in solving people's personal problems (a role traditionally assigned to women, as they are meant to be more empathetic and emotional), rather than as a "negotiator" or "leader."

When the media uses this type of language to describe women and their actions, it paints them as weak and emotional, but nothing in Karen Bass's actual political career hints at weakness. Despite all the criticism and pressure she experienced as the state's leader during our worst economic times, she remained steadfast in her belief in public service. She also did this while dealing with a tremendous personal loss: losing her daughter and son-in-law to a tragic car accident. And, as we saw in Chapter 7, she won a historic victory over Rick Caruso to become mayor of Los Angeles in 2022, despite the enormous amount of money he pumped into his campaign.

Yet, such impressions linger—not only in the minds of fellow politicians, but also in the minds of voters.

During her campaign for mayor, I attended Lt. Governor of California Eleni Kounalakis's "Women for Karen Bass" event. At this event, a woman attending the event asked Karen, "What makes you think you're strong enough to lead Los Angeles?" It's a question that betrays a deeper bias, one that says women may be too "delicate to lead"—a bias helped by the media's use of language.

Women of color face additional barriers of perception and description: Often, Black women are stereotyped as too abrasive, whereas Asian women are too docile to be leaders. These biased public perceptions are a crucial indicator of how much power women will have once they're elected leaders.

Despite tremendous gains in women's representation in powerful positions, people still don't trust women to lead effectively. And it's not just men who think so; many studies have shown that women are just as likely to express disapproval about female leaders as men.

COMPOUNDED BARRIERS FOR WOMEN OF COLOR

Our portrayal in the media is a major contributing factor to why women of color face compounding barriers. We're criticized based on stereotypes about our gender *and* race.

In an MSNBC article, Ja'han Jones highlights this phenomenon, recounting an ignorant and unfounded attack on Vice President Kamala Harris in *The Wall Street Journal* by white female columnist Peggy Noonan. Peggy attacked the first woman vice president—and first woman of color vice president—using unoriginal racist tropes, calling her "unstudious, overly ambitious and too friendly for the role." Ja'han replied, "Suggesting a Black person is lazy while you encourage them to do less work is remarkable evidence of cognitive dissonance."[92]

Ja'han went on to explain that "Black politicians don't need willfully ignorant white journalists humbling them to reach success. They need accurate news coverage, including acknowledgment of all the racist and sexist barriers to success they face. Unfortunately, when members of the press rush to do the former, they inevitably fail to do the latter."

SOCIAL MEDIA

Social media has had countless positive effects on politics and campaigns. It offers voters easy access to candidates' information about their policies and platforms. For candidates, it helps to reach constituents and levels the playing field in campaign fundraising. In addition, social media platforms allow expansive outreach and impact at an affordable cost, as compared to hiring a professional media consultant for a traditional media coverage buy. The opportunities afforded by this technology for women candidates are both positive and meaningful.

However, these benefits are largely overshadowed by the harm social media also causes in the political process. Just as knives and matches were created to be helpful tools, social media can be dangerous and damaging if misused or by individuals with malicious intent.

In 2020, a vindictive rumor about then-vice presidential candidate Kamala Harris spread like wildfire across the social media landscape. Despite her impeccable qualifications as San Francisco's district attorney and California's attorney general, allegations were raised that Kamala actually "slept her way to the top"—one of the oldest, most disgusting, and unimaginative insults one can throw at a successful woman. It shows nothing other than desperation and small-mindedness on the part of the person perpetuating it.

The rumor originated with former California assemblymember Steve Baldwin, who called attention to Kamala Harris's former relationship with then-Assembly Speaker Willie Brown in a post on his personal Facebook page. Steve made the leap to claim Kamala only got to where she was through sexual relationships, such as her past relationship with Willie Brown.

The allegations were false, considering Kamala and Willie's relationship was over for many years before Kamala even ran for an elected office, but the damage was done. Steve Baldwin's implication took on a life of its own. Conservatives scurried out from all the dark corners of the internet to pounce on the morsel. Exaggerated headlines and images were concocted to sensationalize the so-called "story." The hashtag #heelsupharris was used over thirty-five thousand times on Twitter, and Steve's original Facebook post was seen and reshared (with even more offensive extrapolations added) over six hundred and thirty times on Twitter alone.[93]

Just like the seemingly innocent portrayal of women candidates on *SNL*, such slanderous commentary—mainly about a woman's appearance, competence, or personal relationships—cannot be undone once it enters society's subconscious. The sexist perceptions of Kamala Harris were deeply embedded, and nothing could remove them once they were planted.

Beyond its tendency to spread juicy, false information much faster than any benign truths, social media is also a place for people to unleash their most inhumane selves. The "keyboard warrior" can take out all his anger and disappointment on strangers, on topics he knows nothing about. Anyone in the world can make slanderous or disgusting statements, even though such a person would likely shrivel into a prune if they found themselves sitting at a table across from a powerful, intelligent woman like Kamala Harris or Hillary Clinton.

Behind the keyboard, he can call her a bitch, a ditz, or a dominatrix. He can spread lies and make all sorts of statements about her. But with a few exceptions, the average American would never dream of saying such things in the actual presence of the real person.

These sadistic keyboard warriors have turned the otherwise useful tool of social media into a dangerous weapon. Rather than helping spread helpful information and making the political process more effective, they have used social media to derail what little dignity the precarious election process had left.

As of 2023, there were an estimated 4.9 billion social media users worldwide, more than half the world's population.[94] But the dark side of social media can present an enormous risk for women. In particular, women in politics receive an overwhelming amount of online abuse, harassment, and gender bias misinformation on social media platforms.

A recent analysis of the 2020 US congressional races found that women candidates were significantly more likely to experience online abuse than their male counterparts. One example is on Facebook's social media platform, where female Democrats running for public office were the subject of abusive comments ten times more than male Democratic candidates.[95]

Women in politics are disproportionately targeted and victimized by different forms of abuse. These tactics include cyberbullying, trolling, fake news, privacy abuse, and digital harassment, which is becoming a disturbingly regular experience for women. Most male politicians are attacked based on their professional responsibilities, but women politicians are more likely to be attacked related to their physical appearance and humiliating imagery. Women in politics are often targets of disinformation campaigns with misleading or inaccurate information and images. Women who are Asian, minority ethnic, or belong to minority religious groups are more likely to experience online abuse and harassment.[96]

This dark side of social media has unintended consequences for women in politics: it can silence feminist perspectives, discourage women from considering a career in public office, or even push them out of politics. In addition, there are significant privacy issues and psychological harm done to women, including potential threats to their physical safety. The effects of these inflammatory online discussions have real consequences for our democratic process.

Globally, it's been well documented that women in politics are targets of abuse and harassment online. Still, social media companies and governments are not doing enough to hold perpetrators accountable for their actions. Stalking, harassment, death threats, and defamation are prohibited against people, so why is this behavior permitted on social media platforms? How do we take a tougher stance against hate speech, violence, and harassment against women online?

Organizations such as *She Persisted* have made tremendous progress in developing new standards for social media platforms. In 2020, working with Congresswoman Jackie Speier and receiving endorsement by a hundred women lawmakers from over thirty countries, they organized a letter to Facebook/Meta's leadership, urging the company to take action against online abuse towards women in politics.

For now, it seems as though social media is here to stay, with all of its benefits and its pains. It has become a necessary evil for politicians and public figures to understand and learn to live with. Savvy candidates can even find ways to use the resource more to their advantage than disadvantage.

DEALING WITH NEGATIVITY

Negative campaigning is an unfortunate reality for modern American politics. Rather than focusing on the positive attributes of one's candidacy, many candidates decide to simply attack their opponents.

In their report *Men Rule*, researchers Lawless and Fox show that the following deter more women than men: dealing with members of the press (9 percent for women, 6 percent for men), engaging in negative campaigning (28 percent for women, 16 percent for men), and facing a personal loss of privacy (38 percent for women, 29 percent for men).[97] This disparity between men and women is not a matter of toughness. Women are just as tough as men when it comes to withstanding criticism and stomaching false accusations, but for two reasons, the experience is harder for women than for men.

First, public scrutiny tends to be more personal when it comes to women—about her appearance, her tone of voice, what she wears, how she conducts herself as a friend, wife, or mother. The scrutiny of men tends to focus more on their choices and the decisions they make, relevant to the job or campaign in question.

Second, women tend to think collectively about how they impact those around them—their family and their communities. A woman might be willing to withstand extreme scrutiny and even cruelty on a personal level, but if it is impacting those she loves or cares about, she might decide to sacrifice her own ambitions for the good of those around her.

Throughout my career, I've met a broad range of public figures. I've observed many successful politicians who hold their head high, smile, and shake hands even when the media is dragging them through the dirt. I've also met a handful of leaders who unfortunately were affected by these inevitable attacks, to the point that it distracted them from their policy work or even their career path.

The female legislators I interviewed for this book have all been affected by sometimes overblown and inaccurate media reporting, as well as negative campaigning by opponents. So have I. In fact, during my failed Senate campaign, an article surfaced about my male opponent running the most negative campaign in the entire state. One of the many lessons I learned from that experience is the importance of developing toughness—how to block out the noise and rise above the attacks.

When I asked Dr. Lisa Reynolds which was harder, completing medical school or running for public office, she scoffed and declared running for public office was infinitely harder. "In medical school, you know exactly what's expected of you. You must complete XYZ and everyone has the same path to follow in order to complete it. With a political campaign, you have no idea what is going to be thrown at you, what questions or issues you'll have to address, and no two paths are the same." The best you can do is go into it prepared, with thick skin and a good team.

TAKING OWNERSHIP OF THE MEDIA

Candidates have always and will continue to have negative experiences with the media, regardless of the platform. Whether it's hashtags, viral videos, false rumors, unflattering commentary, or flat out lies perpetuated by an opponent's negative campaign, when you step onto the public stage, you will inevitably be scrutinized, fairly or unfairly.

As we've discussed, while almost all politicians experience media coverage, women running or holding public office are scrutinized by their appearance, personality, and family background. Studies have shown that because of online abuse and disinformation campaigns, many women decide against running for public office. What's worse is that, according to Professor Kristina Wilfore, a George Washington University professor and co-founder of the Women's Disinformation Defense Project, women politicians who lead policy areas such as women's rights are more likely to be subjected to such attacks.

Changing the way the media and society as a whole depict women is no simple feat. It is a battle that we've been fighting for decades, and it will not be won any time soon. Just as the centuries-old wealth gap will take generations to overcome, so, too, will the media's deep-seated derogatory depiction of women.

But if we are to break down the imagination barrier, this cultural shift must happen. Women are 51 percent of the population, and we make the majority of buying decisions. We are the commercial market, and with the exception of a few niche outlets, we are news media corporations' target audience. This means that, as consumers, we have the power. By flexing our power, we have the ability to send a loud and clear message to media producers that women demand better.

How do we do this? It's not as simple as holding a rally with special hats; it's deliberate daily choices we make about what and where we give our attention. Push back on social media channels when you see them perpetuating false or derogatory stories. Write to news outlets about their misrepresentation of public female figures. Stop buying from brands or watching channels that fail to progress a positive image of women. As Amanda Hunter of the Barbara Lee Foundation advised, if you hear or see sexist comments, call them out on the spot.

According to *TIME Magazine*, 65 percent of evening broadcasts are led by men and roughly 63 percent of bylines in print and 60 percent online are written by men. Even worse, where women are reporting, they are more likely to report on topics such as lifestyle, culture, and health, whereas men are the ones covering more "important" topics like business, politics, and the economy.[98] This disparity perpetuates society's unconscious bias that men are smarter than women and that men are the ones we should trust when it comes to important matters.

Additionally, men are primarily the ones steering the media ship—occupying the executive producer chair and the editor's desk. They are the ones calling the shots, deciding *what* stories get told and *how* they are told. For this reason, we desperately need more women in these seats. Just as the underrepresentation of women in government has an immensely adverse impact on the development of policies and laws that impact us, our lack of representation in leadership positions in media and entertainment drives how negatively women are depicted in our society.

As Katie Couric said in *Miss-Representation*, "The media can be an instrument of change. It can awaken people and change minds. It depends on who's piloting the plane." We must continue our efforts to take our place in the "pilot seat" of media and entertainment, to control how women are reported on and portrayed.

One of the most significant examples of this positive change is the #MeToo movement. In October of 2017, The New York Times investigative reporters Jodi Kantor and Megan Twohey broke the story of sexual harassment allegations about Harvey Weinstein. Their investigative journalism ultimately helped mobilize and fuel the #MeToo Movement.

As for the media, the solution isn't to fall all over themselves, praising women and their professional accomplishments. We don't need to prohibit the media from ever acknowledging a woman's humanity or femininity. But the absence of commentary about our appearance, our dress, our hair, and our tone of voice would go a long way in allowing viewers to instead focus on what matters: the actual content of our work, our message, and our accomplishments.

I implore the media to focus on substance. It shouldn't matter what color suit the United States Vice President is wearing when she addresses the nation. What matters is what she is saying.

There will come a day in the future when a female politician is discussed in the news for her policy- and decision-making, with no mention of what she was wearing or even acknowledgment of her gender. But this day will not arrive all on its own. The only way we get there is with an overcorrection—acknowledgment of women leaders' successes in parallel recognition of their femininity.

By overtly pointing out instances of women who are successfully leading and responsibly wielding power, we bring to society's attention that the two can, in fact, coexist. This conscious recognition will allow us to tear down the imagination barrier once and for all. And one day, when the imagination barrier no longer exists, we will finally be able to acknowledge a politician's work with no relation to her, his, or their gender.

PART III

ACHIEVING GENDER PARITY

CHAPTER 9

ROLE MODELS, MENTORS, AND ALLIES

"A feminist is anyone who recognizes the equality and full
humanity of women and men. There are many men who are
strong feminists and humanitarians."

—GLORIA STEINEM

When I was twenty-six, I created a national advocacy organization for Asian American women's health. I was naïve about
Asian community politics and had limited skills, but I did have many
mentors and role models for inspiration and guidance.

The early 1990s were an exciting time for women's health. For
example, the National Institutes of Health established the Office of
Research on Women's Health, which went on to launch the first-ever
Women's Health Initiative to combat the most common causes of
death in women. The collective voice advocating women's health issues

at the federal level included healthcare activists Byllye Avery and Julia Scott, co-founders of the National Black Women's Health Project. Around the same time, the National Latina Health Organization was formed by Luz Alvarez-Martinez, working alongside Byllye Avery, to raise consciousness about Latinas' health issues.

Following the example of these women of color healthcare leaders, I organized a group of Asian American women activists, many of whom engaged in research, academia, or social service work within the Asian American community. The first donor to invest in my new non-profit organization was a woman named Jael Silliman.

Julia Scott, the executive director of the National Black Women's Health Project, introduced me to Jael, who was working at the Jessie Smith Noyes Foundation. Jael is a South Asian woman, an incredibly accomplished scholar, and a writer. During our first visit, she asked me, "Where have you been? I've been looking for an Asian American women's health organization to fund." After that, Jael went out of her way to call other foundations and donors on my behalf. I needed that kind of encouragement and guidance in those early days because my financial cushion was thin even without a mortgage.

I was also lucky in having the support of many strong women of color social justice activists, including Pattie Chang of the San Francisco Women's Foundation, Elizabeth Toledo of the National Organization for Women, and Dian Harrison of Planned Parenthood Golden Gate. These women believed that they had a distinct obligation to support other women of color to succeed. At the same time, these mentors, advisers, and friends expected nothing less than hard work and success from me. They needed to know that I fully appreciated these incredible relationships—and I found the best way to reciprocate was to show that I could improve my skills. As a result, I became very good at making the right asks, and understanding what I needed was just as important as knowing what and whom to ask.

Congresswoman Patsy Mink, the first Asian American woman to be elected to the U.S. Congress, served as a vocal advocate for women's rights and Asian American women's health. Her early support helped establish my credibility as an advocate. While serving in Congress, she never turned down my requests for help and often gave me new challenges to further our cause. One of these was organizing a national conference for Asian American women in political leadership, which I did in 1997.

At the time, Patsy was the only Asian American woman in Congress, but there were more Asian American women serving at local levels, like mayors, school boards, and city councils. We had two goals for our conference: first, get locally elected Asian American women officials to become healthcare advocates. And second, build a network of Asian American women in elected office to provide support to one another and to mentor the next generation of leaders.

My role models taught me how to support other women and helped instill in me the idea that helping other women was part of being a true activist. I learned that one of the most impactful things we can do to encourage gender parity is to mentor more women as they enter the political arena.

During my interview with Minnesota State Senator Sandy Pappas, I asked how women can support other women. "Mentor women and vote for women," she responded. This theme was repeated again and again in my interviews with female politicians.

Studies have shown that women who have mentors in the workplace are more successful than women who do not have access to mentors. In a survey of America's 1,250 top executives, every single successful female executive reported having a mentor who used their power to help lift them up.[99] In corporate America, women with mentors rise to positions of power with fewer barriers than women who don't have a mentor. Perhaps this fact explains the gender disparity among top executives: women are 24 percent less likely than men to get advice from senior leaders. 62 percent of women of color lack an influential mentor to help them.[100]

In politics, having a mentor can be a game-changer—they can literally change your career path and life trajectory. In fact, it's common to see legislative staffers who want to succeed their bosses. Cathleen

Galgiani and Fiona Ma, for example, were both mentored by bosses, both of whom were politicians.

In contrast, I was drawn to a particular policy area—mental health—and was fortunate to have met Darrell Steinberg, who invested his time and energy in offering me countless advice and guidance. That's the thing: sometimes mentorship comes from exactly where you hope it will, and sometimes it can come from unexpected places.

NOT EVERY WOMAN WILL SUPPORT YOU

While I found many mentors and role models when I first started out, not everyone I had hoped would support my new endeavor did so. For example, I found opposition from within the Asian American community, since a few older leaders questioned the need for an organization dedicated to gender-specific issues. One of my critics was the executive director at my first job in San Francisco, an Asian woman whom I had worked for several years before launching my organization.

It's rarely acknowledged, but there's a hierarchy within the Asian American community, and long-established leaders like to remain as the gatekeepers. Of course, there's a generational difference too.

My former boss began a whisper campaign, disparaging my limited experience and questioning my motivation, attempting to undercut my confidence. She wasn't successful at stopping my momentum, but she reappeared again and again throughout my career, including during my California State Assembly campaign. This time, she wasn't expressing her aggression covertly; instead, she publicly endorsed my white, male opponent.

There are many reasons why some women do not support other women, and there's no simple answer to explain this phenomenon. One of the barriers is that women are also susceptible to gender bias, including female leaders being biased against their female subordinates. Research suggests that this is because people tend to credit a woman's successes to external factors, such as luck, while viewing her failures as incompetence. At the same time, men are likely to be perceived as leaders when their company succeeds but are less likely to be blamed when their company fails. In addition, our culture celebrates confident and assertive men, while women are socialized to undervalue themselves. Self-promotion is essential for career advancement, but women are likely to be penalized for exhibiting confidence, demonstrating leadership, or sharing their skills and accomplishments.[101]

Some women feel that the competition has limited "spots." They think that there can only be one woman in leadership positions, so they don't want to support other women or they try to adopt a masculine style to fit in. During our interview, Sandy Pappas recalled some of the older women legislators serving with her in the Minnesota State Senate who were focused on not appearing too masculine *and* not appearing too feminine. One female colleague in charge of the Senate Health and Human Services Committee didn't value having other women legislators on her committee, so she didn't let anyone else in.

In her article, *Why Women (Sometimes) Don't Help Other Women*, Marianne Cooper said, "It's not because they're inherently harsher leaders than men, but because they often respond to sexism by trying to distance themselves from other women." Some women use a strategy to "avoid, escape, or navigate the social disadvantage of the group to which they belong" to overcome negative biases held about their group.[102]

Lack of support from other women politicians is not limited to those in the old guard. "Support from female peers? Yes and no," Florida Senate Minority Leader Lauren Book responded with hesitation. "My caucus is wonderful, [but] last November, someone stole my image and created false images of me online. A lot of female members said things like, 'If you weren't so skinny and pretty, this wouldn't happen.' You hope people support you, but they don't. There's a lot of victim blaming."

Another issue is, of course, our "good girl" upbringing. In her groundbreaking book, *Odd Girl Out: The Hidden Culture of Aggression in Girls*, Rachel Simmons details how destructive behavior can be when women are not allowed access to open conflict. "Silence is deeply woven into the fabric of the female experience," she writes.[103] Even in American culture, this behavior was and still is widely promoted among not only Asian girls, but women and girls from all cultural backgrounds.

I did not want to be ruled by the old ways that taught me to be silent. I was determined to move forward. But at age twenty-six, I couldn't comprehend how I could be successful without my former boss's support. It was especially hurtful because I was taught to respect my elders, never talk back, and for the most part, obey the people who are older than me. So, I often turned to Pattie Chang, executive director of The Women's Foundation of California, for guidance and advice.

Pattie had graduated from Stanford Law School and decided to pursue her passion: advocating to end discrimination against women and girls. She helped me realize that my limited view of mentorship was unrealistic. The truth is, women often need more than one mentor, and those relationships must not be one-sided.

MALE ALLIES

When we seek out mentors, female politicians should not only look for other women in power, but should also seek out male allies. My own journey into politics would not have been possible without the support of Sacramento Mayor Darrell Steinberg.

Before I met Darrell, I had worked with many dedicated elected officials through my healthcare advocacy work. Still, working for then-Assemblymember Darrell Steinberg was the first time I could see myself doing the same kind of work, the first time I wanted to change from an advocate to a legislator. Seeing the tangible, wide-sweeping change Darrell's mental health legislation made in people's lives was inspiring.

When I served on the California Mental Health Services and Oversight Commission, Darrell was the Chair of the Commission, which allowed me to have a front-row seat to his consensus-building governance style and his personable leadership skills. For him, it was never about power; it was about making a difference, so he always responded to even his most vocal critics with kindness and compassion. He once said to me, after more than thirty years in politics, "People are free to criticize you. I've gotten better about it, but it still bothers me. But the rewards are immense."

Darrell also helped me understand what this career would demand of me. "Public service is wonderful, but it has to be a choice, and you must understand the sacrifices," he said. "What's the toughest thing about public service? You devote yourself to the public and your causes, leaving less time for family and other personal interests. I've been fortunate to maintain close relationships with my family, but I feel I missed out on some things. I never felt as present as I'd like to be because of the service obligations."

Many of the successful female politicians I've worked with or who I spoke to when writing this book attribute their success to a male mentor. Lauren Book, for example, said that her dad "has always been a role model to me. My mom and sister had mental health issues. I didn't know that women worked and could have important careers. My mom didn't work and was profoundly challenged. So, I always modeled my life after my father."

Lauren said the "love language" between them was work, community service, and activism. "I couldn't do it without my dad. He is a strategic thinker. He sends me law school applications, always pushing me to build capacity and skills. He is my greatest cheerleader. This is a male-dominated field, so you must earn your space."

Lauren's dad was diagnosed with throat cancer, but he is still working in politics and maintaining an active role in her life. "I am always the first one at work, last to leave, and most prepared. He is still working, so we can talk about policy and strategy and have dinner almost every night."

While conversations about mentorship, allyship, and role models are usually about how women should help other women, such as the "Lean-In" message, male mentorship is one of the best strategies to help close the gender gap in politics and achieve political parity. But people with power and connections must be willing to take a chance on women candidates and to help level the playing field for women who often need more resources and links.

There are numerous examples of male mentors changing the game. Condoleezza Rice, the first female African American Secretary of State and the first woman to serve as national security advisor credits former Czech diplomat Josef Korbel, Madeleine Albright's father, for inspiring her to pursue public service. Condoleezza Rice took classes with the former diplomat as an undergraduate at the University of Denver and described her professor, who died in 1977, "as one of the most central figures in my life, next to my parents." At the time of her appointment as Secretary of State, Condoleezza Rice was the highest-ranking woman in the US presidential line of succession.

Similarly, Dr. Jean Fuller, the first female California State Senate Republican Leader, was encouraged by a male elected official to run for state assembly. And Fiona Ma recently tweeted this message about Senator Burton at his birthday party in San Francisco: "I am so grateful he hired me in 1995 as one of his Field Representatives. I believe in fate and being at the right place and right time. Happy 90th Birthday to my Mentor/Boss." Fiona often talks about Senator Burton's mentorship and support, and she credits him for her achievements in politics.

In *Messengers Matter: Why Advancing Gender Equity Requires Male Allies*, a team led by Tarah Williams argued that to achieve gender equality, both women and men must have a role in fighting discrimination. The study found that those men who may not be open to discussing gender equity with women are available to the same message when a man delivers it. In other words, one of the most meaningful actions men can do for gender equity is to confront discrimination and gender bias against women in conversation with other men.[104]

"Leaning in" is not just about what women need to do. It should also place the burden of responsibility on men. Male allies and mentors need to "lean in" to their roles in fighting gender biases in politics.

Darrell acknowledges that his experience differs from women and people of color and that he comes from a place of privilege. "I must support and mentor women," he said. "I feel I have an obligation to help women and people of color. To me, it's part of my responsibility."

PEER MENTORSHIP

Mentorship doesn't only come from older, more established politicians; it can also come from peers. During my campaign for California State Assembly, for example, Sally Lieber was a huge source of support. She spoke up for me within the California Women's Legislative Caucus and helped open doors with Sacramento donors.

Almost every Sunday at 9 p.m., I received a twenty to thirty-page fax from Sally. We were always emailing and faxing each other late at night, and Sally would often extend invitations to swanky networking events to me. She would write, "You need to be at this event," on the faxed pages.

Sally didn't only give me direct support; she also was an important role model for me as I learned the ropes in Sacramento. The third woman to serve as the Speaker ProTem since 1849, Sally was fearless in pursuing her policy goals. She authored the landmark legislation to increase California state's minimum wage and joint-authored a bill to legalize gay marriage with then-Assemblymember Mark Leno. In addition, she championed legislation that provides protections to human trafficking victims and advocated for pregnant inmates in state prisons to be able to deliver their babies without wearing shackles.

She was also fearless in asking for money and votes from strangers. At many events that I'd never heard of, Sally would stand next to the entrance and introduce me to people as they walked by. "Have you met Mary Hayashi, who is running for State Assembly?" she would ask.

Sally's life path to success is an inspiration to women and girls. Her mom stayed home to care for the children and pursued law school when the kids got older, later becoming a paralegal. Her dad had PTSD, but as a former stockbroker, he managed to work as an IRS agent.

After dropping out of high school at sixteen to work as a professional painter, Sally left Detroit when she was just twenty-four years old. She knew some people who had moved to San Francisco from Detroit for better-paying jobs, so she followed in in 1986, arriving a week before Thanksgiving. Her first Thanksgiving dinner in San Francisco was at a local shelter, but she soon got a job in painting and wallpaper installation, which allowed her to start going to school again. She decided to enroll at San Francisco City College.

After meeting her husband, Dave, at a Burning Man concert in 1992, Sally settled in the city of Mountain View. She transferred to Foothill College and became very active in student government affairs, which inspired her to launch a campaign for Mountain View City Council. Her policy platform was to help protect the mobile home park residents. She won the city council as the top vote-getter of seven candidates.

In 2002, Sally ran for the Assembly against Santa Clara City Councilmember Rod Diridon, Jr, a formidable candidate endorsed by most of the Sacramento power brokers and Democratic party officials. But Sally also won that election through grassroots organizing and a small donor fundraising campaign. She said, "For women, we have to overcome obstacles to running, and even more challenges await when you're elected to a male-dominated institution like the state legislature." Because Sally didn't have much support from women legislators when she was a candidate for state assembly, she was determined to help other women candidates who run for office.

Sally is not alone in supporting her peers as they navigate the world of politics. Lauren Book supports other candidates—and uses her position as minority leader to hire women into powerful support roles. For example, she hired the first female Latina chief of staff in the Florida legislature, Maggie Gerson, who is a former prosecutor with a reputation for being tough and savvy.

Sometimes, Maggie would look at her boss and mumble, "Don't you cry!" because Lauren was prone to crying during floor speeches. "She supports me and gets it," Lauren said. "You want to bring those women along, so we are supporting each other. I am proud to have a mostly female staff."

At the time of our interview, Lauren was actively working on getting another woman elected: first-generation Cuban American Jeanelle Parez, who was running for Florida State Senate in Miami. Lauren gets exhausted from all the work that requires her attention, but helping candidates like Jeanelle keeps her going. She thinks it's important to have diversity in the legislature and for people who "look like her" to see her. Women mentoring women in politics is a powerful tool.

Elected officials can be ideal peer mentors to women candidates because they have a wealth of knowledge about the campaign process, as well as legislative experience and access to powerful networks sometimes only available to incumbents. Peer mentoring can be particularly crucial for first-time women candidates.

CREATING A PATH FORWARD

During my first campaign for the California State Assembly, I reached out to then-San Francisco district attorney Kamala Harris for her endorsement. She invited me to meet her for lunch at Lulu in San Francisco, where I talked about my personal background and my motivation for running for assembly. Before I got to the endorsement question of the conversation, she interrupted and said, "I am endorsing you." It felt amazing to earn her support for my first political campaign. It was a powerful endorsement—and a confidence booster.

Sixteen years later, watching Kamala Harris, the first female vice president, walk onto the stage at Mayor-Elect Karen Bass's inauguration event, I felt so grateful to live in a country where we value role models like Kamala Harris. For women and girls to be able to see a future for themselves in politics, it's important for them to see these successful women.

I've learned over the years that mentorship isn't one-sided or exclusive, nor is it something you need only early in your career. For example, though Darrell was a huge supporter when I first entered politics, he couldn't endorse me for my state senate campaign because he happened to be the leader of the Senate, and he had close ties to other candidates running in my race.

As we transition jobs and transform who we are, we must expand our network of allies and mentors—of any age or gender. It's about being open to engaging your peers and looking for an opportunity to learn from people who have accomplished the goals you hope to achieve. People who can be a sounding board, who share their experiences and wisdom and who challenge your thinking. I would not have won my campaign for state assembly without the other women and men who helped guide me.

Self-doubt, gender stereotypes, and biases prevent many women and girls from pursuing politics, but a true representative democracy must include women in policy- and decision-making. We must build strong women's mentorship opportunities, where all elected officials and political and community leaders effectively promote gender equality. We must continue to engage our male allies and mentors, who can advocate for women and help them gain access to opportunities in a male-dominated political environment.

Research suggests that having women in powerful positions can inspire other women, and exposure to positive women role models helps reduce the implicit biases that women may hold.[105] Mentors, allies, and role models all play an essential role in helping to achieve political parity. Through our journeys, we will continue to be inspired and benefited by the many women and men who chose to make a difference in people's lives. In turn, it's up to us to create our legacy by shaping the paths of others.

CHAPTER 10

BEING THE CHANGE YOU WANT TO SEE

"Each time a woman stands up for herself, without knowing it possibly, without claiming it, she stands up for all women."

—MAYA ANGELOU

I n 1983, Joyce ("Sunny") Mojonnier was elected to the California State Assembly's seventy-fifth district. She was the thirtieth woman ever elected to California's assembly, and at the time, there were only eleven women out of eighty members.

"Back then, it was still very much a boy's club," Sunny recalled during my interview with her. "We weren't allowed into the Sutter Club"—Sacramento's historical meeting place for California politicians and lobbyists—"but instead of fighting to prove we belonged in their club, I eliminated the glass ceiling by starting our club!"

The same year that she was elected to the state assembly, Sunny founded the Capitol Network, a private organization for female legislative and administrative professionals serving California's government. The Capitol Network celebrated its birth with a private party that has since become famous in many political circles. About sixty female members of California's senate, assembly, lobbyists, and press corps attended the dinner at Sunny's condo in downtown Sacramento, mingling over beers while commiserating about defeated legislation and innocuous sexual harassment.

But the night's highlight was the few brave male colleagues who were there by special invitation. Assembly Speaker Willie Brown, Assembly Minority Leader Bob Naylor, Senators Jim Ellis and Art Torres, and Dave Sterling from the Governor's office served as bartenders and waitstaff for the women.

The press wrote numerous stories about the groundbreaking event. One local paper described a compelling conversation overheard amongst the partygoers:

"It may be 'progressive' California, they said, but each had her stories of fending off advances, being the brunt of rumors, and enduring patronizing airs. It may have improved simply because more women are being elected, appointed and hired. But the improvements won't be noticeable, they were agreeing, until the numbers increase even more—until a generation has passed and what is now a minority of men, comfortable with women as equals, becomes the majority of men."[106]

Well, it's been thirty years since Sunny and her peers celebrated the establishment of The Capitol Network. Since then, the number of women in elected office has increased, but the question they posed in 1983 remains: Are the improvements noticeable? And while *most* men are now comfortable with women as their equals, why aren't *all* men comfortable? Do we have to simply wait longer for the rest of them to "come around?"

The originally proposed solution also remains true: The only way to make real change is for more women to hold office and positions of power. As time passes, new generations of men will grow up in a world where they regularly interact with women as their peers. We are making progress toward this future, but all of the resources and the mentoring in the world can't change things unless women step up to the plate.

Because of our "good girl" nature, we usually look to find a way to fit into existing systems. We've been doing this for decades now, working our way into networks and organizations that men built. But we are half of the world's population. We have ten times the consumer buying power of men. We are now even more educated than our male peers.

We can build our networks. We can draw from each other's energy, donate to each other's campaigns, and lift each other. We can continue to insert ourselves into the good-ole boy networks, but we must also forge our own.

Let's talk about how we can go about becoming the change we want to see in the world, one individual at a time.

STRIVE FOR AUTHENTICITY

In my experience supporting women politicians, I've also noticed that younger women running for and taking office, like Senator Lauren Book, are more willing to share their personal stories. This may be because they grew up with social media, or simply with the message that our differences should be celebrated rather than hidden. In any case, today's generation embraces transparency while politicians from older generations are typically more guarded. Being vulnerable takes courage, but it also makes a candidate more relatable, showing voters that she understands the importance of the issues.

So, I want to emphasize the importance of authenticity. There is no better example than Connie Perez-Andreesen, a CPA and former congressional candidate for CD 21. Born in the city of

Tulare to Mexican immigrant parents, Connie came from humble beginnings. Connie and her family lived at the Woodville Farm Labor Camp in California, where her father worked on a farm. The Woodville Farm Labor Camp is within California's Central Valley, about eight miles west of Porterville and eighteen miles southeast of Tulare. Farm workers, who form the backbone of the US's $164 billion agricultural industry, are paradoxically among the poorest workers, earning wages that are inadequate to support a family.[107] They often work in dangerous conditions, risking their health, safety, and education opportunities. Farm workers are regularly exposed to pesticides, sometimes die from heat stress, and often lack access to clean drinking water. The government data also shows that many of the agricultural workers who have died from these working conditions were foreign-born.[108]

Connie grew up watching her father work on farms in the Coachella Valley and neighboring areas. She is a product of the Head Start Program. She graduated from Monache High School, attended Bakersfield College, and graduated Magna Cum Laude in 2000 from California State University, Bakersfield (CSUB), with a degree in business administration. In 2002, through her hard work and dedication—sometimes overcoming what many told her was impossible—Connie became a certified public accountant.

Growing up in the Woodville Farm Labor Camp, there weren't many activities for kids; everyone simply hung out at a big park nearby. Connie, like many other children in the area, had never met anyone who had attended college, was often surrounded by drug dealers, and gang violence posed a perpetual threat. Tragically, the summer before her graduation, Connie's younger brother Jesus, who was involved with drug cartels and struggled with substance and alcohol abuse, was shot and killed. He was only nineteen years old, and his death left his one-year-old son, Fernando, without a father. Reeling from this devastating loss, Connie and her family made the decision to become Fernando's legal guardians.

Connie started as a staff accountant at a regional accounting firm based in Kern County, becoming one of only two Latinas to make partner in its forty-year history. She had accomplished something many living at the Woodville Farm Labor camp could only dream of. But she felt something was missing. "I often thought about the farmworkers left behind at the labor camp. Although I had fulfilled the dream of becoming an accountant, I wanted to make a difference in the lives of others."

In September 2015, Connie's career took an unexpected turn. The Democratic Congressional Campaign Committee (DCCC), led by former Speaker Nancy Pelosi, discovered her potential. They persuaded Connie to consider a new path: running for Congress. Invigorated by the idea of making an even bigger impact and helping people, Connie decided to take the plunge.

Connie's campaign consultants had some political advice for her: "Don't be seen alone with a man anywhere because you're a single female. Do not wear too much makeup when attending a community function. And dress appropriately—no short skirts or shorts." Their advice came from experience. For example, a female local state legislator was captured on camera smoking a cigar with several male colleagues, and this photo resurfaced as a negative attack mailer during her subsequent campaigns. Of course, none of the male colleagues smoking cigars with the local female legislators received negative feedback.

"So much about campaigning for public office had to do with style over substance," Connie recalled. "I loved that [Alexandria Ocasio-Cortez] could wear her hair long and wear bright lipstick. She is authentic, and voters accept the way she is."

Connie's campaign consultants also told her she needed to raise $300,000 as soon as possible. Connie explained, "I am not a wealthy person, but I had to pay for my travel expenses to Washington, DC, to raise campaign funds. I felt overwhelmed and unprepared—I have community events fundraising experience, but never had to make cold calls asking strangers for $2,900 for a political campaign." Connie shared with me her hopes that women's candidate training programs will soon reach the Central Valley part of the state. She feels that formal training programs can benefit many untapped talents and candidates in that part of the region.

In October 2015, Connie issued the following statement to the press: "After careful consideration of all the factors, including my family, business, and public service commitments to the boards and commissions that I serve, I have decided not to pursue my candidacy at this time in my career. I will continue to work tirelessly to improve the lives of the residents in the Central Valley, as I always have." So, Connie suspended her congressional campaign.

Connie did not return to a for-profit accounting firm. Instead, following her congressional campaign, Connie pursued her passion for public service by becoming the controller for the United Farm Workers of America (UFW). The UFW is America's first and largest farm workers' union, founded in the early 1960s by Cesar Chavez, Dolores Huerta, and other organizers. The union's National Executive Board promoted her to serve as the UFW's Chief Administrative Officer in 2018 and National Vice President at the UFW Constitutional Convention in November 2020.

Connie has no regrets about quitting her congressional campaign. She is now working on many landmark public policy initiatives to protect all California farm workers, especially at non-union ranches. "The UFW is a leader in the national movement for immigration reform. Its most recent reform bill for immigrant field workers passed the US House, and the union continues to champion legislative reforms for farm workers, covering issues such as overtime, heat safety, other worker protections, and pesticides." Connie continues volunteering with an array of non-profit and community organizations. She has been recently named CSUB Foundation Chair and was inducted into the CSUB Hall of Fame in 2022.

Although no longer a political candidate, Connie strived for authenticity. Her courage to participate in a congressional campaign and her decision to end the campaign when she no longer felt authentic ultimately allowed her to follow the public service path she had always dreamt of.

Many highly regarded politicians in history were viewed as authentic. Regardless of gender, race, political party, or voting record, authenticity is invaluable and women like Connie serve as an important reminder and role model for women in politics.

BEYOND THE "GOOD GIRL"

When I entered politics, I found the "good girl" habits I was raised with were tough to break. They were not an issue in my early career, when I advocated for Asian Americans. However, as a candidate running for public office, I had to advocate for myself. That was something I had never done before. I had no idea how to tactfully speak about my accomplishments and tout myself as a potential leader. I was raised to never speak my mind, challenge others, or self-promote. Instead, I was taught to place great care in what others thought of me. As a result, I was highly uncomfortable asking strangers for money through campaign donations.

I knew these behaviors wouldn't bode well for someone in public office, and overcoming them is an ongoing process. To this day, I get nervous speaking up and voicing my perspective in public. I question the value of what I say, how others perceive me, and if I'm a "good girl." But I continue to challenge myself to push past these traits and embrace my "strong girl" persona.

Throughout this process, a helpful strategy I employed was to emulate leaders I respected. These leaders were both women and men—not due to preference, but simply because men constituted the majority in the state legislature and in all other political circles I was involved with. As I watched them and modeled behaviors I admired, I began to speak my mind freely, became confident when presenting my position, referenced my credentials and experience to support my arguments, and debated respectfully. With practice, adopting their mannerisms eventually became natural.

Most importantly, while I worked to expand my comfort zone, I remained authentic. I continued to be polite and friendly but learned to balance these traits with strength and confidence. While my colleagues weren't used to seeing strength and confidence from an Asian woman, my mannerisms were familiar, so they at least knew how to respond. This was better than having them encounter a timid and hesitant Asian woman, a stereotype they would be more familiar with but would not respect or partner with.

It's important to understand that adjusting one's presentation or behavior is not a version of selling out. Rather, it is more like learning a language. It is a matter of knowing one's audience and finding an appropriate version of yourself to present. As Amanda Hunter said during our interview, "Is it fair that we must make these adjustments? No, but we must remember the goal right now is to get more women elected to leadership positions. Hopefully, we will no longer have to make such adjustments over time as white men will no longer dominate the landscape."

OPPORTUNITIES FOR WOMEN

The systemic barriers of wealth and influence that women face when running for office are greatly multiplied when they run against an incumbent, particularly a male. Not only does she have the imagination barrier working against her, but donor confidence is practically zero for a candidate facing an incumbent.

This is why open-seat contests are such significant opportunities for women. According to CAWP, Ballotpedia found that fewer than 5 percent of incumbents lost their bids for reelection in 2020. That same year, four-fifths of newly elected women (or 389 out of 476) won open-seat contests.[109]

Women must look for and capitalize on such opportunities, as this helps high-potential candidates get a "foot in the door." Organizations like EMILY's List and Emerge America can help female candidates identify open-seat contests and guide them in preparation for winning these races. And a woman with a foot in the door can hold it open for other women who choose to follow her in.

Women are also learning more about fundraising directly from each other. Before her congressional race, while she was still speaker of the California Assembly, Karen Bass convened a meeting of all the state's women legislators to discuss how we could become better fundraisers. During the session, we took turns discussing some of our most significant fundraising challenges. Those in the group, like Fiona Ma, who were very successful fundraisers shared their best practices. The meeting felt like a step forward for gender parity in government and was a huge win for peer-to-peer mentorship because the purpose was "we," not "me." Each helpful lesson and word of encouragement added to the foundation first set by women like Sunny Mojonnier back in 1983.

You don't have to be independently wealthy or an experienced fundraiser to fund a campaign successfully. Women must get creative to compete with male candidates who take a more traditional approach to campaign financing. Even so, as a participant in that meeting, my eyes were opened to the various resources available to women candidates and the unique fundraising advantages we have over men.

PERSISTENCE IS CRUCIAL

In 2008, Sally Liber was termed out of the state assembly. She ran for state senate in 2012 and 2020 but lost both elections after enduring bruising attacks by her male opponents. In early 2022, she made a decision to run again—this time as a member of the California State Tax Board of Equalization. Sally won that three-way race, taking 53 percent in the June primary.

Often, women candidates face questions about their qualifications and likeability after losing a campaign, and many feel that running again may not be a viable career path for them. Many are discouraged by their negative campaign or social media experiences. But Sally's courage to run again after losing two consecutive campaigns demonstrates that women candidates are just as tough and resilient as their male counterparts.

Previous studies suggest that women are more likely to leave politics after a losing campaign than men for many reasons, including but not limited to women being more risk-averse and more likely to dislike fierce competition. But a groundbreaking study by political scientists from Harvard Kennedy School and the University of California, Davis contradicted these claims.

In a comprehensive research study, Justin de Benedictis-Kessner and Rachel Bernhard examined whether or not 213,966 men and women candidates decided to run again after losing a campaign. This study looked at state legislative races; California county, city, and school district elections; and mayoral elections from 1950 through 2018, and it involved a total of 22,519 jurisdictions. Among the key findings was that there are no significant gender differences in candidates' responses to losing their elections. For example, in state legislative races, men who lost were 38 percent less likely to run again than those who won their races. For women, 39 percent were less likely to run again after losing.[110]

"Contrary to fears expressed by pundits and scholars alike, the potential for many women candidates to be driven from politics due to losing (relative to men) appears to be unfounded," said Justin de Benedictis-Kessner and Rachel Bernhard. Rachel added, "Once women overcome the barriers of running for office in the first place, they are just as likely to persist as men."

The authors explained that the number of women candidates running since the 2016 Presidential election has increased dramatically, but many of them running for the first time lost at higher rates than men. "We hope that these results will be encouraging for the people and organizations who are investing in women and working to get more women in office," Rachel said. "While there is a lot of work to be done to get to gender equality in politics, this study shows that those investments aren't lost even when women lose elections."

In 1997, State Senator Sandy Pappas ran for Mayor of St. Paul. She was the Democratic-Farmer-Labor endorsed candidate, but she lost to Norm Coleman in the November run-off election. In 2000, she passed on the chance to run for Congress because she hadn't recovered from the intensity of the 1997 mayoral race. In my interview with her, Sandy said that someone once told her it takes at least seven years to recover from an election loss.

When I met Sandy in 2014, she was serving as the Senate President of the Minnesota State Senate. Sandy's initial motivation for running for office was heavily influenced by a series of social justice movements: the civil rights and anti-war movements in the late 60s and early 70s. In sixth grade, she wrote an essay on what it means to be an American, quoting John F. Kennedy's famous line, "Ask not what your country can do for you but what you can do for your country." From that moment, she was aware of her interest in public service.

Sandy's parents divorced when she was young, and she remembers the housing challenges her family experienced as a result. When Sandy was sixteen years old, helping raise her younger two siblings, her dad lost his job and stopped paying child support, so she started working. She spent time as a union organizer at a grocery store but was fired one day for wearing a button that said, "We share the dream." As a teenager, she considered Martin Luther King Jr. a role model.

In the 1970s, Sandy began her activism by participating in the American Indian Movement and protesting the Vietnam War. Though she became an active anti-war advocate, women weren't allowed in organizing or strategy sessions back then. She and other women activists made coffee for everyone and provided administrative support to the male activists engaged in organizing strategies. So, when the women's movement started, she was all over it. And in 1972, when

Sandy attended the first women's march in New York, it changed her life.

After Sandy married her husband and moved to Minnesota, she continued her community activism. She joined a local food co-op and became the board chair. She also joined a feminist theater group that produced their shows.

One day when their third child was on the way, Sandy's husband was talking about the pending election and their horrible choices for the state legislature. He suggested she should run for the State Legislature, and she joked that her campaign slogan could be "She will deliver" since she was expecting. But that joke turned into her actually running in 1982.

Sandy's first campaign didn't do very well, so she decided to drop out. When she announced that she was quitting in front of the party officials, she received a standing ovation. Democratic party leaders were impressed with her drive and appreciated Sandy's graciousness.

Sandy spent the following two years planning and preparing for the next state representative campaign, and in 1984 she won with the party's endorsement. In 1990, she was recruited to run against an anti-labor incumbent state senator. She did and won the senate seat.

The underrepresentation of women in the public and private sectors feeds on itself. I share the realities of these barriers not to discourage women from entering politics but to help women understand what we're up against. While there are many obstacles, these examples demonstrate that women can overcome them. The more women overcome them, the smaller these barriers will become until one day, as Sunny and her dinner guests envisioned thirty years ago, they become non-existent.

So, persist. No matter how high the barriers may seem now or how difficult it is, persist. Create and lean on the network around you to build a new world, one with a more equitable distribution of power, wealth and influence, one that represents the change you want to see.

CHAPTER 11

NEXT GENERATION OF WOMEN LEADERS

**"I believe the rights of women and girls
is the unfinished business of the 21st Century."**

—HILLARY CLINTON

We've come a long way since the early 1970s when just a handful of women held political leadership positions. Since the 2016 presidential election, we have seen a record number of women running for public office. Although many political experts have attributed this surge to Donald Trump's presidency, author Sarah Kuta of the University of Colorado, Boulder, speculates that Hillary Clinton inspired many more women to pay attention and run for office.[111]

When women run for high-profile public office, that directly impacts women and girls' ability to imagine that they can do the same. As the first woman to be nominated by a major party for president, Hillary Clinton is a role model for the next generation of female candidates for the highest office in the country, but we must remember that it takes time to break down cultural and systemic barriers. "Often, the pioneers who clear the paths do not have the honor or privilege of running along them," Faye Wattleton, former president of Planned Parenthood Federation of America, said. "If it's not Mrs. Clinton who becomes our first [female] president, she will have made an enormous contribution."[112] Four years after Hillary Clinton ran for president, we saw more women candidates declaring and running for President, including Elizabeth Warren, Kamala Harris, Amy Klobuchar, and Kirsten Gillibrand.

The November 2022 election cycle was an important turning point for women in politics for a couple of reasons. First, we made history with a record number of women winning and now serving in Congress, state legislatures, and executive positions.[113] Second, and more importantly, many of these women are now holding key leadership positions, including eighteen women who hold the top leadership position in their chamber, such as State Senate President or Speaker of the House.[114] These opportunities are critical because women in leadership positions can influence the state's legislative agendas, prioritize its state spending and develop gender-specific public policy initiatives.

According to the Center for American Women in Politics at Rutgers University, a record number of women are currently serving as governors (24 percent, or twelve, women governors) and serving in the US Congress (28.7 percent, or one hundred and twenty-five, of the House is women, and there are twenty-five women in the Senate). In the state legislatures, women now hold 32.7 percent of all seats.[115]

Today, 49 percent of lieutenant governors in the United States are women. The Barbara Lee Family Foundation recently released a report, *Second in Command,* proving that voters perceive lieutenant governors to be qualified to serve as governors.[116] What's more?

Three states elected their *first* woman governor in 2022: Arkansas, Massachusetts, and New York. Governors Maura Healy (D-MA) and Tina Kotek (D-OR) became the first openly lesbian women to serve as governors. In addition, fifty of the California legislature's 120 legislators are women.

It's important to note that, during the November 2022 election cycle, a record number of women were represented in both the candidacy and nomination stages. Twenty-five women ran for governor across twenty states, and in Oregon, all three major parties nominated women candidates: Democratic, Republican, and Independent. In Oakland, Sheng Thao, a daughter of refugees who fled Laos during a genocide, made history as the youngest ever elected to serve the city as mayor—and the first Hmong American woman elected. Throughout her campaign, she often spoke about escaping an abusive relationship and living out of her car with her infant son, challenging preconceptions of what an elected official is supposed to be. The increase in women candidates, party nominees and winners all contribute to the growth of women's representation and inspire other women to see themselves as potential women elected officials.

The statistics are slowly moving toward equitable representation, but we still have a way to go. The number of women serving is an all-time high but still short of the 50 percent necessary for gender parity. In the executive branch, only 24 percent of governors are female, 25.1 percent of cities with a population over 30,000 have female mayors, and while we finally have our first female vice president of the United States, we have yet to elect a woman as president. In the state legislature, only 32.7 percent of women serve even though we make up 51 percent of the population.

As discussed in Chapter 7, there is still a lack of racial and ethnic diversity among women officeholders across all positions, especially at the gubernatorial level.

The success of women candidates in our future elections will be achieved by concerted recruitment efforts, supporting women candidates with fundraising, and breaking down the cultural and racial barriers. Otherwise, we will not be able to sustain and ensure continued progress toward gender parity.

MILLENNIALS AND GENERATION Z: RESHAPING AMERICAN POLITICS

While generations of cultural, systemic, and racial barriers take time to break down and overcome, the next generation of women leaders—participating in national, local, and community leadership roles—will have significant turning points in American politics.

According to a 2016 Pew Research Center report, Millennials and Generation Z hold similar views on politics, as well as more liberal views than older generations. The majority of those surveyed say that racial and ethnic diversity is a good thing, compared to the older generation who are less convinced. These younger generations believe that Black people are treated less fairly than white people in the United States and tend to view same-sex marriage favorably.[117] In particular, Generation Z has been greatly influenced by Donald Trump's presidency, a global pandemic, protests over police violence, and attacks on women's reproductive rights. They are expected to be the most well-educated and racially/ethnically diverse generation yet.

David Hogg, a survivor of the 2018 shooting at Marjory Stoneman Douglas High School in Parkland, Florida, launched a new PAC focused on recruiting and supporting young candidates for public office. David and his co-founder Kevin Lata launched Leaders We Deserve to help Gen Z candidates around the country get elected to state legislatures and the US Congress. And in a recent joint press interview with David, Kevin said, "We will be the EMILY's List for young people."

What's more, since the 2016 election, EMILY's List has received more than four thousand inquiries from women candidates interested in running. Emerge America, a non-profit candidate recruitment and training organization, has seen an average increase in applications of 87 percent. In her interview with the *Christian Science Monitor*, Andrea Dew Steele, president and founder of Emerge America, said, "We have never seen this kind of interest in running for office. We spend a lot of time begging women to run for office. This is unusual: to get women interested without trying to recruit them with numerous conversations."[118]

Elise Stefanik is one millennial politician who is shaping the future of American politics. In 2014, at age thirty, she made history as the youngest woman ever to have been elected to Congress up to that point. No Republican had won her district (27th District of New York) in twenty-one years.

Despite her opponent questioning her qualifications and resume, she won 61 percent of the vote in the primary and 55 percent against the Democratic nominee in November. In her victory speech on election night, she said to the media, "I am honored and humbled to be the youngest woman ever elected to the United States Congress and to add an additional crack to the glass ceiling for future generations of women here tonight."

As the first woman to serve as Recruitment Chair for the National Republican Congressional Committee, Elise Stefanik successfully recruited more than one hundred women during the 2022 election cycle, leading the national effort to recruit and mentor Republican women candidates. "I am going to keep pointing out to my colleagues that we are at a crisis level for GOP women," Elise said in an interview with Politico on December 11, 2018. "This election should be a wake-up call to Republicans that we need to do better…We need to be elevating women's voices, not suppressing them."[119] After facing opposition to her efforts to diversify the Republican caucus from male colleagues, Elise responded via tweet that she "wasn't asking permission" to make the necessary changes within the Republican Party.

LOOKING AHEAD

Today, we are confronted with some of the most daunting social and cultural crises in generations. Scientists have warned that our planet is suffering a crisis of mass extinction on a scale unseen since the dinosaurs. Global warming poses a serious threat to life on Earth, and scientists are urging immediate and radical action. More than any other time, many working people cannot afford housing, leaving them homeless or facing eviction. In fact, Millennials are expected to be the first generation in decades to earn less than their parents. And since the COVID-19 pandemic, mental illness and demand for help are at an all-time high among children and teens, though we are simultaneously experiencing an unprecedented shortage of healthcare professionals. Finally, the US has a higher income inequality gap than other advanced economies, and that gap is growing even more rapidly in recent years.

At the global level, we can see the dramatic social and economic outcomes of extreme gender disparity. In its *Global Gender Gap Report 2022*, the World Economic Forum analyzed four areas: economic participation, education attainment, health, and political representation. The results showed that it will take 132 years to reach full gender parity at the current pace.[120]

Research and anecdotal evidence both provide clear evidence that women's political participation advances complex and emerging public policy issues, as well as results in diverse strategies for social and economic problems. Women in politics also affects the public policy issues prioritized in government, as we have seen in states like Nevada. As Barbara Lee, founder and president of the Barbara Lee Family Foundation, so eloquently stated, "Women don't run for office to seek fame and fortune. They run for office to solve problems."

Throughout my journey, both as a participant in the political landscape and as an author, I've been privileged to delve deep into the diverse experiences of women in politics. Their representation is not just about sheer numbers but also the rich diversity of experiences and perspectives women bring to the table. And so, in writing this book, I embarked on numerous interviews, anticipating a broad spectrum of narratives.

However, to my surprise, a common thread emerged—across races, across age groups, so many of these women have faced strikingly similar challenges and barriers. Their stories underscore a universal truth: Women, irrespective of their backgrounds, encounter similar, particular hurdles in their political journeys. This revelation emphasized even more fervently why women's representation in the political realm is so important.

Throughout history, women have grappled with systemic gender discrimination, often amplified in the political arena. But what makes their representation so paramount is the unique lens through which women view societal issues, rooted in their multifaceted roles as caregivers, professionals, mothers, and community leaders. Women often approach problems with a holistic mindset, seeking collaborative solutions that benefit the broader community. Their distinct approach is born from a blend of life experiences, including oppression, that men simply don't share.

Yet, the path isn't easy. The myriad challenges women face, from battling stereotypes to overcoming deep-seated biases, can deter many competent and passionate candidates. This makes it even more crucial for stories of perseverance, like those I've collected, to come to the forefront. By sharing these struggles and triumphs, we not only inspire future generations but also highlight the dire need for creating an environment that's more welcoming and supportive of female leadership.

When women occupy political spaces, they not only represent half of the population but also advocate for issues that might otherwise be overlooked or undervalued. They challenge entrenched power structures, ushering in a more inclusive and egalitarian political environment. All the women I interviewed for this book, from those who have paved the way in the past to the trailblazers of today, consistently emphasized their commitment to service and problem-solving. Their narratives are a testament to the indispensable role of women in the political landscape, reinforcing the idea that when women lead, society as a whole progresses.

Representation matters. It's essential that we empower women and girls to take active roles in politics, reinforcing the belief that they can, and should, become influential leaders within their communities and beyond. Traditional markers of candidacy, such as experience in local governance, personal affluence, an education from elite institutions, or family connections, no longer define the archetype for public service. I challenge these outdated notions of what an elected official should be. And even if the battle is uphill, with the right support, women candidates remain undeterred by electoral setbacks. They rise, run again, *win*, and navigate the myriad systemic, racial, gendered, and cultural obstacles that stand in their way.

We all have a role to play in changing the look of leadership in our world, one elected office at a time, and an increasing involvement of women in politics paves the way for more inclusive, accountable, and open democracies.

In reflecting upon the experiences and insights shared throughout this book, one truth emerges with profound and undeniable clarity—a truth that has always existed, but perhaps was never so starkly evident. For our democracy to genuinely reflect the diversity of its citizens, the active involvement of women in the political sphere is not just a hopeful aspiration or welcome addition. It is an essential cornerstone of a truly representative democracy.

ACKNOWLEDGMENTS

First and foremost, I would like to express my heartfelt gratitude to all the women legislators, mentors, and thought leaders who generously provided their time and support in making this book possible. Thank you for sharing your wisdom and lessons with me. I am incredibly grateful for your inspiring personal journeys and leadership stories. This book cannot capture all of the complexities of women in politics, but I have made every effort to represent events as faithfully as possible, including contacting all copyright holders to ensure the information in this book was correct at the time of publication.

My sincere thanks to Mariel Hemingway for providing the inspirational foreword for my book. Writing *Women in Politics* was much more complicated than I thought, and it was only possible with my publishing team's support and guidance. I am thankful to everyone who has provided inspiration, advice, and resources in the writing of my second book: Karen Bass, Lauren Book, Laphonza Butler, Sue Chan, Rosemary Dyer, Jean Fuller, Cathleen Galgiani, Jennifer Glover, Haylee Gordon, Giselle Hale, Olivia Hammerman, Dallas Harris, Amanda Hunter, Celinda Lake, Sally Lieber, Fiona Ma, Sunny Mojonnier, Sandy Pappas, Connie Perez-Andreesen, Lisa Reynolds, Sharon Reis, Cindy Ryu, Darrell Steinberg, Sally Giddens Stephenson, Victoria Stewart, and Alex Vassar.

A special thanks to the Center for American Women and Politics (CAWP) of the Eagleton Institute of Politics at Rutgers, The State

University of New Jersey, for providing the incredible body of research and current data about women's political participation in the United States. Their dedication to promoting greater knowledge about the role of American women in politics has made a huge difference in the lives of people we serve. And thanks to all the amazing work of the Barbara Lee Family Foundation for showing us what is possible.

This book would not exist without the willingness of my friends and colleagues to share their experiences and support. True friends are hard to come by, and I am fortunate to have had friends who stood by me during every struggle and all my successes. I am forever indebted to Elizabeth Healy, who is always there to support me, and Scott Gunn, who makes me laugh and lifts my spirits. And special thanks to those who help me succeed in politics: Leticia Alejandrez, Jim Anderson, Byllye Avery, Craig Bueno, Sue Chan, Robin Chin, Garrett Contreras, Kitty Dana, Hal Dasinger, Anna Eshoo, Donna Gerber, Afton Hirohama, Phong La, Sally Lieber, Mike Paiva, Chris Parman, Richie Ross, Julia Scott, Liz Snow, Elizabeth Toledo, Ross Warren, Kathy Wat, and Dan Weitzman. Because of their efforts and advice, I have a legacy to pass on to future women legislators contemplating elective office.

I am thankful every day for my husband, Dennis, a constant role model and inspiration. Thank you for always being the person I can count on. And special thanks to my loyal family members who encouraged me to face new challenges: Cindy, Peter, Gary, and Dee. Finally, I treasure my nephews, Nick, John, Kevin, and Brian—the children in my life and the best teachers I could ever have. Thank you.

ABOUT THE AUTHOR

Mary Chung Hayashi is an award-winning author, national health-care leader, and former California State Assemblymember. With a distinguished career in public service, Mary has spearheaded substantial reforms in mental health services, championed gender equality, and forged powerful, unprecedented partnerships for social causes that previously had no financial or public backing. Recognized as "Legislator of the Year" by the American Red Cross and the California Medical Association, Mary has also been featured on *Redbook*'s "Mothers and Shakers" list and *Ladies' Home Journal*'s "Women to Watch." As Principal of Public Policy & Advocacy Solutions, she has successfully advised business and policy leaders on some of today's most complex public policy matters. Mary remains a steadfast proponent of social justice expansion and the rights of underrepresented communities.

ENDNOTES

1   Robert Nilsen, *Moon Handbook: South Korea*, 4th ed. (New York: Avalon Travel, 2009), 551.

2   Allison O'Connor and Jeanne Batalova, "Korean Immigrants in the United States," *Migration Information Source*, Migration Policy Institute, April 10, 2019, https://www.migrationpolicy. org/article/korean-immigrants-united-states-2017.

3   Kelly Dittmar et al., *Representation Matters: Women in the U.S. Congress* (New Brunswick, NJ: Center for American Women and Politics, Eagleton Institute of Politics, Rutgers, the State University of New Jersey, 2017), 11–17, https://cawp.rutgers. edu/sites/default/files/resources/representationmatters.pdf.

4   Sarah Ewall-Wice, "Record Number of Women Are Running for Governor and Winning Their Primaries," CBS News, August 25, 2022, https://www.cbsnews.com/news/record-number-of-women-are-running-for-governor-and-winning-their-primaries/.

5   Edwin Ng and Carles Muntaner, "The Effect of Women in Government on Population Health: An Ecological Analysis among Canadian Provinces, 1976–2009," *SSM—Population Health* 6 (December 2018): 141–148, https://doi.org/10.1016 /j.ssmph.2018.08.003.

6 Sarah F. Anzia and Christopher R. Berry, "The Jackie (and Jill) Robinson Effect: Why Do Congresswomen Outperform Congressmen?," *American Journal of Political Science* 55, no. 3 (July 2011): 478–493, https://doi.org/10.1111/j.1540-5907.2011.00512.x.

7 Merissa Khurma et al., *Ready to Lead: Understanding Women's Public Leadership in the Middle East and North Africa* (Washington, DC: Wilson Center, 2020), 32, https://www.wilsoncenter.org/sites/default/files/media/uploads/documents/MEP_2002_MENA%20report_v2_Corrected_0.pdf.

8 Kantar, *The Reykjavik Index for Leadership: Measuring Perceptions of Equality for Men and Women in Leadership: 2020–2021* (London: Kantar, n.d.), 78, https://www.kantar.com/campaigns/reykjavik-index.

9 "Legislative Advocacy," Lauren's Kids, accessed August 2, 2023, https://laurenskids.org/advocacy/legislation/.

10 Lauren's Kids, "Legislative Advocacy."

11 Missing or Unidentified Persons, S.B. 1066, California State Senate 2013–2014 Regular Session (2014), https://openstates.org/ca/bills/20132014/SB1066/.

12 KXTV Staff, "Missing Person Files Go Mission in San Joaquin Sheriff's Office," ABC10, March 10, 2015, https://www.abc10.com/article/news/local/stockton/missing-person-files-go-missing-in-san-joaquin-sheriffs-office/103-183455347.

[13] Kelly Dittmar et al., *Representation Matters: Women in the U.S. Congress* (New Brunswick, NJ: Center for American Women and Politics, Eagleton Institute of Politics, Rutgers, the State University of New Jersey, 2017), 6, https://cawp.rutgers.edu/sites/default/files/resources/representationmatters.pdf.

[14] Tax Exemption for Diapers and Incontinence Products, S.B. 246, Florida Senate 2022 Session (2022), https://www.flsenate.gov/Session/Bill/2022/246/?Tab=BillHistory.

[15] Ted Gregory, "Tarana Burke Discusses Her Me Too Movement, Hollywood's Hashtag Co-Opting of It," *UChicago News*, March 29, 2023, https://news.uchicago.edu/story/tarana-burke-discusses-her-me-too-movement-hollywoods-hashtag-co-opting-it.

[16] *New Research: Voters, Candidates, and #MeToo* (Cambridge, MA: Barbara Lee Family Foundation, April 2018), 1–2, https://www.barbaraleefoundation.org/wp-content/uploads/Memo-How-Voters-Feel-About-MeToo.pdf.

[17] Kate Abbey-Lambertz, "Lawmaker Bravely Reveals She Was Victim of Rape in Emotional 'Abortion Insurance' Debate," HuffPost, updated January 23, 2014, https://www.huffpost.com/entry/gretchen-whitmer-rape_n_4432203.

[18] Emily Shugerman, "The #MeToo Movement Takes Office after Winning Elections across the U.S.," Daily Beast, updated November 7, 2018, https://www.thedailybeast.com/the-metoo-movement-takes-office-after-winning-elections-across-the-us.

[19] Brenda Clubine, "Convicted Women against Abuse Fact Sheet," Sin by Silence, accessed August 2, 2023, http://www.sinbysilence.com/pressmaterials/cwaafacts.html.

[20] Michele L. Swers, *The Difference Women Make: The Policy Impact of Women in Congress* (Chicago: The University of Chicago Press, 2002); Michele L. Swers, *Women in the Club: Gender and Policy Making in the Senate* (Chicago: The University of Chicago Press, 2013).

[21] Caroline Dobuzinskis, "One on One with Professor and Expert on Women in Politics, Dr. Michele L. Swers," Institute for Women's Policy Research, May 2, 2013, https://iwpr.org/one-on-one-with-professor-and-expert-on-women-in-politics-dr-michele-l-swers/.

[22] U.S. Centers for Disease Control and Prevention, "Cigarette Smoking among Adults—United States, 1994," *Morbidity and Mortality Weekly Report* 45, no. 27 (July 12, 1996): 558–590, https://www.cdc.gov/mmwr/preview/mmwrhtml/00042976.htm.

[23] Carly Sauvageau, "Nevada Likely to Remain Top State for Most Women in Legislature," *The Nevada Independent*, September 18, 2022, https://thenevadaindependent.com/article/nevada-likely-to-remain-top-state-for-most-women-in-state-legislature.

[24] Helier Cheung, "Did First Female-Majority Legislature in US Make a Difference?," BBC News, March 4, 2020, https://www.bbc.com/news/world-us-canada-51623420.

[25] Amanda Hunter, "Dismantling the 'Imagination Barrier,'" Gender on the Ballot, September 29, 2021, https://www.genderontheballot.org/dismantling-the-imagination-barrier/.

[26] Christine Ro, "Why Do We Still Distrust Women Leaders?," Equality Matters—How We Work, BBC, January 19, 2021, https://www.bbc.com/worklife/article/20210108-why-do-we-still-distrust-women-leaders.

[27] Jennifer L. Lawless and Richard L. Fox, *Men Rule: The Continued Under-Representation of Women in U.S. Politics* (Washington, DC: Women & Politics Institute, 2012), 9, https://www.american.edu/spa/wpi/upload/2012-men-rule-report-final-web.pdf.

[28] Tara Sophia Mohr, "Why Women Don't Apply for Jobs Unless They're 100% Qualified," *Harvard Business Review*, August 25, 2014, https://hbr.org/2014/08/why-women-dont-apply-for-jobs-unless-theyre-100-qualified.

[29] Jennifer L. Lawless and Richard L. Fox, *Girls Just Wanna Not Run: The Gender Gap in Young Americans' Political Ambitions* (Washington, DC: Women & Politics Institute, 2013), 8, https://www.american.edu/spa/wpi/upload/girls-just-wanna-not-run_policy-report.pdf.

[30] Lawless and Fox, *Girls Just Wanna*, ii.

[31] Kira Sanbonmatsu, Susan J. Carroll, and Debbie Walsh, *Poised to Run: Women's Pathways to the State Legislatures* (New Brunswick, NJ: Center for American Women and Politics, Eagleton Institute of Politics, Rutgers, the State University of New Jersey, 2009), 8, https://cawp.rutgers.edu/sites/default/files/resources/poisedtorun_0.pdf.

[32] Emma Goldberg, "Nightly Applause Is Nice, but Some Doctors Think Votes Would Be Nicer," *The New York Times*, May 9, 2020, https://www.nytimes.com/2020/05/09/us/politics/doctor-politicians-coronavirus.html.

[33] Lawless and Fox, *Men Rule*, 10–11.

[34] Sanbonmatsu, Carroll, and Walsh, *Poised to Run*, 8-10.

35 Sanbonmatsu, Carroll, and Walsh, *Poised to Run*, 11–14.

36 Sarah Jane Glynn, *An Unequal Division of Labor: How Equitable Workplace Policies Would Benefit Working Mothers* (Washington, DC: Center for American Progress, 2018), 3, https://www. americanprogress.org/wp-content/uploads/sites/2/2018/05/ Parent-Time-Use.pdf.

37 Glynn, *An Unequal Division*, 17–18.

38 Kelly Dittmar, Kira Sanbonmatsu, and Susan J. Carroll, *A Seat at the Table: Congresswomen's Perspectives on Why Their Presence Matters* (New York: Oxford University Press, 2018), 78.

39 Gretchen Livingston, "Stay-at-Home Moms and Dads Account for about One-in-Five U.S. Parents," Pew Research Center, September 24, 2018, https://www.pewresearch.org/fact-tank/2018/09/24/stay-at-home-moms-and-dads-account-for-about-one-in-five-u-s-parents/.

40 Jennifer L. Lawless and Richard L. Fox, *Men Rule: The Continued Under-Representation of Women in U.S. Politics* (Washington, DC: Women & Politics Institute, 2012), 11, https://www.american. edu/spa/wpi/upload/2012-men-rule-report-final-web.pdf.

41 Jennifer L. Lawless and Richard L. Fox, *Girls Just Wanna Not Run: The Gender Gap in Young Americans' Political Ambitions* (Washington, DC: Women & Politics Institute, 2013), 16, https://www.american.edu/spa/wpi/upload/girls-just-wanna-not-run_policy-report.pdf.

42 Lawless and Fox, *Men Rule*, 6.

43 Dittmar, Sanbonmatsu, and Carroll, *A Seat at the Table*, 79.

44 Kira Sanbonmatsu and Claire Gothreau, *The Money Race for the State Legislature: Individual Contributions, 2020* (New Brunswick, NJ: Center for Women and Politics, Eagleton Institute of Politics, Rutgers University, 2021), 17, https://cawp.rutgers.edu/sites/default/files/resources/cawp_money_race.pdf.

45 "House, Senate and Presidential Candidate Registration," Federal Election Commission, accessed August 2, 2023, https://www.fec.gov/help-candidates-and-committees/registering-candidate/house-senate-president-candidate-registration/.

46 Liz Halloran, "Mother of Women's PACs Seeks Younger Supporters: EMILY's List, Then and Now," NPR, April 29, 2010, https://www.npr.org/templates/story/story.php?storyId=126393558.

47 "Distribution of Billionaires in the United States in 2022, by Gender," Statista, April 5, 2023, https://www.statista.com/statistics/1125817/billionaires-united-states-distribution-gender/.

48 Robert Reich and Heather McCulloch, "Op-Ed: Wealth, Not Just Wages, Is the Way to Measure Women's Equality," *Los Angeles Times*, August 25, 2017, https://www.latimes.com/opinion/op-ed/la-oe-reich-mcculloch-womens-wealth-gap-20170825-story.html.

49 Sanbonmatsu and Gothreau, *The Money Race*, 22.

50 "In 2020 Women Ran, Won and Donated in Record Numbers," OpenSecrets, December 21, 2020, https://www.opensecrets.org/news/2020/12/women-ran-won-donate-record-numbers-2020-nimp/.

51 Justin Wolfers, "Fewer Women Run Big Companies Than Men Named John," *The New York Times*, March 2, 2015, https://www.nytimes.com/2015/03/03/upshot/fewer-women-run-big-companies-than-men-named-john.html.

52 Claire Cain Miller, Kevin Quealy, and Margot Sanger-Katz, "The Top Jobs Where Women Are Outnumbered by Men Named John," *The New York Times*, April 24, 2018, https://www.nytimes.com/interactive/2018/04/24/upshot/women-and-men-named-john.html.

53 Karen O'Connor, *Gender and Women's Leadership: A Reference Handbook* (Los Angeles: Sage Reference, 2010), 152; Fredreka Schouten, "EMILY's List Raises Record $90 Million," *USA Today*, January 10, 2017, https://www.usatoday.com/story/news/politics/onpolitics/2017/01/10/emilys-list-raises-record-90-million
/96391160/.

54 Federal Election Commission, "Number of Federal PACs Increases," press release, August 12, 2008, https://www.fec.gov/updates/number-of-federal-pacs-increases-2/.

55 "Top 20 PACs to Candidates, 2017–2018," OpenSecrets, accessed August 2, 2023, https://www.opensecrets.org/political-action-committees-pacs/top-pacs/2018.

56 Kira Sanbonmatsu, Susan J. Carroll, and Debbie Walsh, *Poised to Run: Women's Pathways to the State Legislatures* (New Brunswick, NJ: Center for American Women and Politics, Eagleton Institute of Politics, Rutgers, the State University of New Jersey, 2009), 4, https://cawp.rutgers.edu/sites/default/files/resources/poisedtorun_0.pdf.

57 *Keys to Elected Office: The Essential Guide for Women* (Cambridge, MA: Barbara Lee Family Foundation, 2021), 24, https://www.barbaraleefoundation.org/wp-content/uploads/Keys-to-Elected-Office_Final.pdf.

58 Kira Sanbonmatsu and Claire Gothreau, *The Money Race for the State Legislature: Individual Contributions, 2020* (New Brunswick, NJ: Center for Women and Politics, Eagleton Institute of Politics, Rutgers University, 2021), 17, https://cawp.rutgers.edu/sites/default/files/resources/cawp_money_race.pdf.

59 Grace Haley and Sarah Bryner, "Which Women Can Run? The Fundraising Gap in the 2020 Elections' Competitive Primaries," OpenSecrets, June 9, 2021, https://www.opensecrets.org/news/reports/2020-gender-race.

60 Haley and Bryner, "Which Women."

61 Angela Yang, "From Crime Victims to Politicians, Misidentifying Asians Is Part of America's Racist History," NBC News, March 1, 2022, https://www.nbcnews.com/news/asian-america/crime-victims-politicians-misidentifying-asians-part-americas-racist-h-rcna17218.

62 Yang, "From Crime Victims to Politicians."

63 "'You All Look Alike to Me' Is Hard-Wired in Us, Research Finds: Less Differentiation in Other-Race Facial Features Occurs in the Earlies Cognitive Processes," ScienceDaily, July 8, 2019, https://www.sciencedaily.com/releases/2019/07/190708112419.htm.

64 Yang, "From Crime Victims to Politicians."

[65] Aba Osseo-Asare et al., "Minority Resident Physicians' Views on the Role of Race/Ethnicity in Their Training Experiences in the Workplace," *JAMA Network Open* 1, no. 5 (2018): e182723, https://doi.org/10.1001/jamanetworkopen.2018.2723.

[66] Zulekha Nathoo, "Why People of Colour Are Misidentified So Often," Equality Matters—How We Work, BBC, May 25, 2021, https://www.bbc.com/worklife/article/20210519-why-people-of-colour-are-misidentified-so-often.

[67] Nathoo, "Why People."

[68] *STAATUS Index Report 2021* (San Francisco: LAAUNCH, 2021), 30, https://assets.website-files.com/6390f08a537fe1d7185850f5/6390f08a537fe150a75851b1_staatus-index-2021-final.pdf.

[69] *STAATUS Index Report 2021*, 3.

[70] LAAUNCH, *STAATUS Index 2023: Attitudes towards Asian Americans and Pacific Islanders* (San Francisco: The Asian American Foundation, 2023), 6, https://staatus-index.s3.amazonaws.com/2023/STAATUS_Index_2023.pdf.

[71] Jessica Guynn and Jayme Fraser, "Exclusive: Asian Women Are Shut Out of Leadership at America's Top Companies. Our Data Shows Why," *USA Today*, April 25, 2022, https://www.usatoday.com/story/money/2022/04/25/asian-women-executives-discrimination-us-companies/7308310001/?gnt-cfr=1.

[72] "Latinas Aren't Paid Fairly—And That's Just the Tip of the Iceberg," Lean In, accessed August 2, 2023, https://leanin.org/data-about-the-gender-pay-gap-for-latinas.

[73] "Indicator 19: College Participation Rates," National Center for Education Statistics, last modified February 2019, https://nces.ed.gov/programs/raceindicators/indicator_REA.asp; Lean In, "Latinas Aren't Paid."

[74] Lean In, "Latinas Aren't Paid"; Ruta Yemane and Mariña Fernández-Reino, "Latinos in the United States and in Spain: The Impact of Ethnic Group Stereotypes on Labour Market Outcomes," *Journal of Ethnic and Migration Studies* 47, no. 6 (2021): 1240–1260, https://doi.org/10.1080/1369183X.2019.1622806.

[75] Lean In, "Latinas Aren't Paid"; Colleen Flaherty, "(More) Bias in Science Hiring," Inside Higher Ed, June 6, 2019, https://www.insidehighered.com/news/2019/06/07/new-study-finds-discrimination-against-women-and-racial-minorities-hiring-sciences; Kate Bahn and Will McGrew, "The Intersectional Wage Gaps Faced by Latina Women in the United States," Washington Center for Equitable Growth, November 1, 2018, https://equitablegrowth.org/the-intersectional-wage-gaps-faced-by-latina-women-in-the-united-states/.

[76] Jasmine Tucker, *55 Cents on the Dollar Isn't Enough for Latinas*, Fact Sheet (Washington, DC: National Women's Law Center, October 2020), 1–3, https://nwlc.org/wp-content/uploads/2019/11/Latina-EPD-2020.pdf.

[77] Tucker, *55 Cents*, 1–3.

[78] Daphna Motro et al., "The 'Angry Black Woman' Stereotype at Work," *Harvard Business Review*, January 31, 2022, https://hbr.org/2022/01/the-angry-black-woman-stereotype-at-work.

[79] Sharon Epperson, "Black Women Make Nearly $1 Million Less Than White Men during Their Careers," CNBC, August 3, 2021, https://www.cnbc.com/2021/08/03/black-women-make-1-million-less-than-white-men-during-their-careers.html.

[80] Jasmine Tucker, *Native American Women Need Action That Closes the Wage Gap*, Fact Sheet (Washington, DC: National Women's Law Center, September 2021), 1, https://nwlc.org/wp-content/uploads/2020/09/Native-Women-Equal-Pay-2021.pdf.

[81] Kira Sanbonmatsu, Susan J. Carroll, and Debbie Walsh, *Poised to Run: Women's Pathways to the State Legislatures* (New Brunswick, NJ: Center for American Women and Politics, Eagleton Institute of Politics, Rutgers, the State University of New Jersey, 2009), 10, https://cawp.rutgers.edu/sites/default/files/resources/poisedtorun_0.pdf.

[82] Jewel L. Prestage, "Black Women State Legislators: A Profile," in *A Portrait of Marginality: The Political Behavior of the American Woman*, eds. Marianne Githens and Jewel L. Prestage (New York: David McKay Company, 1977), 401–418.

[83] Deena Zaru, "On the Money: How 3 Women of Color Overcame a Broken System and Made History in Congress," Good Morning America, October 23, 2020, https://www.goodmorningamerica.com/news/story/money-women-color-overcame-broken-system-made-history-73692457.

[84] Sanbonmatsu and Gothreau, *The Money Race*, 5; "QuickFacts: United States," U.S. Census Bureau, accessed August 2, 2023, https://www.census.gov/quickfacts/fact/table/US/PST045222.

85 "Women Elected Officials," Center for American Women and Politics, accessed August 2, 2023, https://cawpdata.rutgers.edu/women-elected-officials/.

86 Faith Karimi, "In the Nearly 232-Year History of the US Senate There Have Only Been 11 Black Senators," CNN, January 25, 2021, https://www.cnn.com/2021/01/25/us/black-us-senators-history-trnd/index.html.

87 Lauren Aratani, "Record Number of Native American Women Elected to Congress," *The Guardian*, November 4, 2020, https://www.theguardian.com/us-news/2020/nov/04/native-american-women-elected-congress-record-number; CAWP Staff, "Asian or Pacific Islander (API) and Middle Eastern or North African (MENA) Women Candidates in 2020," Center for American Women and Politics, August 5, 2020, https://cawp.rutgers.edu/blog/asian-or-pacific-islander-api-and-middle-eastern-or-north-african-mena-women-candidates-2020.

88 Center for American Women and Politics, "Women Elected Officials."

89 Amanda Fortini, "The 'Bitch' and the 'Ditz,'" *New York Magazine*, November 14, 2008, https://nymag.com/news/politics/nationalinterest/52184/.

90 *Miss Representation*, written and directed by Jennifer Siebel Newsom (Ross, CA: Girls' Club Entertainment, January 22, 2011), 85 min., https://therepproject.org/films/miss-representation/.

91 Eric Bailey, "A Target atop the Assembly," *Los Angeles Times*, July 8, 2009, https://www.latimes.com/archives/la-xpm-2009-jul-08-me-karen-bass8-story.html.

92 Ja'han Jones, "How White Journalists Fail in Their Coverage of Vice President Kamala Harris," *The ReidOut Blog*, MSNBC, December 14, 2021, https://www.msnbc.com/the-reidout/ reidout-blog/kamala-harris-criticism-media-rcna8712.

93 Karen Tumulty, Kate Woodsome, and Sergio Peçanha, "How Sexist, Racist Attacks on Kamala Harris Have Spread Online—A Case Study," *The Washington Post*, October 7, 2020, https://www.washingtonpost.com/opinions/2020/10/07/ kamala-harris-sexist-racist-attacks-spread-online/.

94 Belle Wong, "Top Social Media Statistics and Trends of 2023," *Forbes*, May 18, 2023, https://www.forbes.com/advisor/ business/social-media-statistics/.

95 Cécile Guerin and Eisha Maharasingam-Shah, *Public Figures, Public Rage: Candidate Abuse on Social Media* (London: Institute for Strategic Dialogue, 2020), 17, https://www.isdglobal.org/wp- content/uploads/2020/10/Public-Figures-Public-Rage-4.pdf.

96 Lucina Di Meco and Saskia Brechenmacher, "Tackling Online Abuse and Disinformation Targeting Women in Politics," Carnegie Endowment for International Peace, November 30, 2020, https:// carnegieendowment.org/2020/11/30/tackling-online-abuse-and- disinformation-targeting-women-in-politics-pub-83331.

97 Jennifer L. Lawless and Richard L. Fox, *Men Rule: The Continued Under-Representation of Women in U.S. Politics* (Washington, DC: Women & Politics Institute, 2012), 11, https://www.american. edu/spa/wpi/upload/2012-men-rule-report-final-web.pdf.

98 Alexandra Sifferlin, "The Media Is (Still) Dominated by Men," *Time*, April 3, 2014, https://time.com/48170/ the-media-is-still-dominated-by-men/.

99 Carla Carlini, "What the World Needs Now Is More Women Mentors," *Forbes*, October 3, 2017, https://www.forbes.com/sites/womensmedia/2017/10/03/what-the-world-needs-now-is-more-women-mentors/?sh=27cfc0c96465.

100 "Men Commit to Mentor Women: Not Harassing Women Is Not Enough," Lean In, accessed August 2, 2023, https://leanin.org/mentor-her.

101 Yasmine Kalkstein and Kimberly Kopack, "How Implicit Biases Complicate Female Mentorship," Decision Lab, December 27, 2020, https://thedecisionlab.com/insights/hr/how-implicit-biases-complicate-female-mentorship.

102 Marianne Cooper, "Why Women (Sometimes) Don't Help Other Women," *The Atlantic*, June 23, 2016, https://www.theatlantic.com/business/archive/2016/06/queen-bee/488144/.

103 Rachel Simmons, *Odd Girl Out: The Hidden Culture of Aggression in Girls* (New York: Harcourt, 2002), 3.

104 Tarah Williams et al., "Messengers Matter: Why Advancing Gender Equity Requires Male Allies," *PS: Political Science & Politics* 54, no. 3 (2021): 512–513, https://doi.org/10.1017/S1049096521000093.

105 Danielle M. Young et al., "The Influence of Female Role Models on Women's Implicit Science Cognitions," *Psychology of Women Quarterly* 37, no. 3 (2013): 283–292, https://doi.org/10.1177/0361684313482109.

106 Sunny Mojonnier, "Capitol Network—In the Beginning," Capitol Network, accessed August 2, 2023, http://www.sunnymojonnier.com/capitol-network-in-the-beginning/.

[107] Kathleen Kassel and Anikka Martin, "Ag and Food Sectors and the Economy," Economic Research Service, U.S. Department of Agriculture, last modified January 26, 2023, https://www.ers.usda.gov/data-products/ag-and-food-statistics-charting-the-essentials/ag-and-food-sectors-and-the-economy/.

[108] According to the National Institute for Occupational Safety and Health, the farm worker fatality rate averaged four heat-related deaths per one million workers per year, which is twenty times higher than the 0.2 rate for U.S workers overall. (Larry L. Jackson and Howard R. Rosenberg, "Preventing Heat-Related Illness among Agricultural Workers," *Journal of Agromedicine* 15, no. 3 (2010): 200–215, https://doi.org/10.1080/10599 24X.2010.487021.)

[109] Kira Sanbonmatsu and Claire Gothreau, *The Money Race for the State Legislature: Individual Contributions, 2020* (New Brunswick, NJ: Center for Women and Politics, Eagleton Institute of Politics, Rutgers University, 2021), 18, https://cawp.rutgers.edu/sites/default/files/resources/cawp_money_race.pdf.

[110] Rachel Bernhard and Justin de Benedictis-Kessner, "Men and Women Candidates Are Similarly Persistent after Losing Elections," *Proceedings of the National Academy of Sciences* 118, no. 26 (2021): e2026726118, https://doi.org/10.1073/pnas.2026726118.

[111] Sarah Kuta, "Women Who Run for Office Inspire Others to Do the Same, Study Suggests," *Colorado Arts and Sciences Magazine*, July 31, 2018, https://www.colorado.edu/asmagazine/2018/07/31/women-who-run-office-inspire-others-do-same-study-suggests.

112 Jeet Heer, "Hillary Clinton's Legacy Is Huge and Lasting: Far from Being a Historical Footnote, She's a Pathbreaking Pioneer," *The New Republic*, September 14, 2017, https://newrepublic. com/article/144796/hillary-clintons-legacy-huge-lasting.

113 "Women in Elective Office 2023," Center for American Women and Politics, accessed August 2, 2023, https://cawp.rutgers.edu/ facts/current-numbers/women-elective-office-2023.

114 Kelly Dittmar, "Women in Election 2022: Making Midterm Progress: State Legislatures," Center for American Women and Politics, accessed August 7, 2023, https://womenrun.rutgers. edu/2022-report/state-legislatures/.

115 Center for American Women and Politics, "Women in Elective Office 2023."

116 *Second in Command: The Challenges and Opportunities Facing Women Lieutenant Governors* (Cambridge, MA: Barbara Lee Family Foundation, 2023), 2, https://www. barbaraleefoundation.org/wp-content/uploads/2023-BLFF-Lt.-Governors-Research-SECOND-IN-COMMAND.pdf.

117 Kim Parker, Nikki Graf, and Ruth Igielnik, "Generation Z Looks a Lot Like Millennials on Key Social and Political Issues," Pew Research Center, January 17, 2019, https://www. pewresearch.org/social-trends/2019/01/17/generation-z-looks-a-lot-like-millennials-on-key-social-and-political-issues/.

118 Story Hinckley, "Surge in Young Women Planning to Run for Office," *The Christian Science Monitor*, February 2, 2017, https://www.csmonitor.com/USA/Politics/2017/0202/ Surge-in-young-women-planning-to-run-for-office.

119 Rachael Bade and Sarah Ferris, "'I Wasn't Asking for Permission': GOP Women Put Leaders on Notice," Politico, December 11, 2018, https://www.politico.com/story/2018/12/11/gop-women-leadership-1055195.

120 Kusum Kali Pal et al., *Global Gender Gap Report 2022*, Insight Report (Geneva: World Economic Forum, 2022), 5, https://www.weforum.org/reports/global-gender-gap-report-2022/digest.